# EASY TO COOK

# SALADS

## Meg Jansz

ANAYA PUBLISHERS LTD
LONDON

First published in Great Britain in 1994 by
ANAYA PUBLISHERS LTD.
Strode House, 44-50 Osnaburgh Street, London NW1 3ND

Design and art direction by Patrick McLeavey & Partners, London

**Photographer**: Patrick McLeavey
**Home Economist**: Meg Jansz
**Photographic Stylist**: Patrick McLeavey
**Editor**: Alison Leach

British Library Cataloguing in Publication Data
Jansz, Meg
Easy to cook salads. – (Easy to cook)

ISBN 1–85470–162–2

Typeset by Bookworm Typesetting, Manchester
Colour reproduction by Scantrans Pte Ltd, Singapore
Printed in Portugal by Printer Portuguesa Lda

NOTES
Ingredients are listed in metric, imperial and cup
measurements.
Use one set of quantities as they are not
interchangeable.

All spoon measures are level:
1 tablespoon = one 15ml spoon
1 teaspoon = one 5ml spoon.

Use fresh herbs and freshly ground black pepper
unless otherwise stated.

Use standard size 3 eggs unless otherwise
suggested.

Throughout this book 'Preparation time' refers to the time required
to prepare the ingredients. It does not include time for cooking,
soaking, marinading etc, which is given in the recipe method.

# CONTENTS

Gone are the days of a limp lettuce leaf, tomato and cucumber partnering a slice of ham on a plate. With so many unusual salad and herb leaves featuring on our supermarket shelves, the salad lover has a constantly growing source of inspiration for creating new salads.

Add to this leafy base the huge variety of other vegetables, pulses, meats, cheeses, seafoods, fruits and nuts available to us, and you can create an infinite number of salads to suit every taste and occasion.

Most salads make for healthy eating because whatever you add to them, their basic ingredients are raw vegetables that retain their vitamins and minerals. These being water soluble, would otherwise be lost in cooking. Raw food generally, and ingredients like nuts and dried fruit in particular, also help to provide the fibre necessary for a healthy diet.

For the health conscious, *Easy to Cook Salads* contains chapters on fresh and healthy salads and grains, beans and pasta. The eleven *Fresh and Healthy* recipes use light dressings and ingredients such as fruit, tofu and low fat fromage frais and yoghurt. The twelve salads based on *Grains, Beans and Pasta* whilst not necessarily low in calories, are high fibre recipes which can be eaten as meals in themselves.

Salad days do not necessarily spell "D-I-E-T". Nor do they have to end with the onset of winter. *Easy to Cook Salads* contains recipes that can be enjoyed in every season, whether you are counting calories or being a little self-indulgent. Besides classic favourites such as *Salad Niçoise* and *Caesar Salad* and some unusually dressed side salads, you can try original main courses like *Crispy Duck and Mango Salad* or go for something spicy and exotic like *Bombay Salad*, a combination of courgettes and blanched broccoli with toasted cashew nuts and coconut, finished with a curry-flavoured dressing.

Much fresh produce, despite year-round availability is still best in its proper season. For example try *Salad Elona* in June when English strawberries are at their best both in flavour and value for money. *Summer Herb and Flower Salad* is a visually stunning salad, an ideal choice for our summer months when fresh herbs, varied salad leaves and edible summer flowers such as borage are plentiful. Similarly, use abundant pears in autumn to make *Pear, Stilton and Walnut Salad*. Other recipes like *Chick Pea and Chorizo Sausage Salad* or *Gadoh-Gadoh*

which use dried, storecupboard or exotic ingredients, will taste just as good the whole year round.

Whether using seasonal or store cupboard ingredients, it is essential for these to be of high quality. This is especially true when preparing simple, easy to cook recipes and when, as in this book, many ingredients are used raw. Crisp and fresh produce can make all the difference between a flavoursome or a mediocre salad.

As well as buying good quality ingredients, the storage and treatment of them is important. Always store salad vegetables in a cool, dark place, ideally in the vegetable drawer of your refrigerator. Direct sunlight and heat deteriorates the vitamin content of vegetables as well as making them limp and unattractive.

Nuts are an important element of many of my recipes, because they partner salad vegetables so well and are also an excellent source of fibre. Due to their high oil content they do not have a good shelf life so should be bought in small quantities, stored in an airtight container in a cool place and used within a few weeks. To help bring out their flavour, they can be toasted before use, as described in the relevant recipes.

Another tip is to always dry washed salad leaves before dressing them. This keeps them crisp and makes it easier for the salad dressing to coat the leaves. For frequent salad-makers, a salad spinner is a worthwhile addition to your kitchen because it is the quickest and most effective way of drying leaves.

Preparing and eating food should not simply be a necessity for survival, but rather an enjoyable experience. Consequently, presentation of the food is important to create visual appeal. Salad ingredients with their tantalising variety of colours and textures, are the perfect medium for doing just this. Again freshness is vital for presenting appetising and attractive salads. The vibrant photography in *Easy to Cook Salads* captures the way in which a wide variety of different crisp leaves combined with the red and orange of tomatoes, purple onions and the green and white hues of spring onions can provide limitless opportunities to provide a feast for the eyes and the appetite. Imagine yellow, green and orange peppers contrasting with the differing textures of black olives, roasted pecan nuts, young asparagus spears, soft goat's cheese and delicate quails's eggs all tossed lightly in glistening oils and aromatic herbs. To enhance the aesthetic appeal, leaves can be torn, herbs snipped and vegetables attractively sliced. Those few extra moments spent arranging the salad can make all the difference.

Dressings, that other vital element of any good salad, should complement the tastes of the main ingredients and not dominate or disguise them. With all oil and vinegar dressings the proportion of oil to vinegar is ultimately a matter of personal taste, but the classic ratio is one part vinegar to three parts oil.

Oils are used in virtually all salad dressings and the most frequently used are olive oil, virgin olive oil, sunflower, grapeseed, hazelnut and walnut oils. It is generally accepted that some are more healthy than others – olive oil being a monosaturate is the ideal choice for cholestrol watchers, whilst the nut oils, although not so healthy, are nonetheless delicious.

Most of the *Easy to Cook Salads* have oil-based dressings, but do experiment with varying the suggested oils (and vinegars) to create your own version of a salad.

Oils do not have a long shelf life and if kept for too long will go rancid. Buy them in quantities appropriate to your needs. Likewise, avoid storing vinegars for long periods as they become cloudy and very acidic.

Vinegar is a frequent partner of oil in salad dressings. White wine, red wine, tarragon, cider and balsamic vinegars are the most widely used, but there is also a large variety of other flavoured vinegars ranging from champagne, sherry and rice wine vinegar to shop-bought ones with added herbs and spices.

It is easy to make this choice virtually infinite by flavouring both oils and vinegars yourself. For example, to make a spicy olive oil, add dried chillies, garlic cloves, black peppercorns and sprigs of rosemary to olive oil or add chives, lemon rind and fennel seeds to sunflower oil and fresh basil sprigs to extra virgin oil.

You can flavour your own vinegars too. Some examples are oregano and pink peppercorns in red wine vinegar, chervil and orange rind in champagne vinegar, mint sprigs in white wine vinegar and sage and red onion slices in cider vinegar. These home-prepared flavoured oils and vinegars should be kept in a sunny place for two weeks before use, to allow the flavours to develop. Fruit can also be used to sweeten vinegars:

## STRAWBERRY OR RASPBERRY VINEGAR
Place 450g (1lb) washed strawberries or raspberries in a large bowl and crush lightly. Pour over 600ml (1pt) white wine vinegar. Cover the bowl with cling film and leave for 4 days, stirring once a day. Strain liquid through muslin into a saucepan and add 75g (3oz) caster sugar. Heat gently till sugar has dissolved, then boil for 1 minute. Cool slightly and pour fruit vinegar into sterilised bottles. Seal and leave to mature for 3 weeks. Fruit vinegars are best used within 6 months of preparation.

## QUICK FRUIT VINAIGRETTE
Mango or Peach Vinaigrette is an unusual but easy dressing. It must be kept refrigerated and used within a few days of preparation. Place the flesh from 1 ripe, peeled mango or 1 large ripe peach in a food processor. Add 2 tablespoons white wine vinegar and 5 tablespoons grapeseed oil. Season with salt and pepper. Puree till the mixture is thick and smooth. These dressings are good served with cold meats and smoked chicken. Alternatively add a tablespoon of chopped dill or coriander and serve them with smoked fish or cooked prawns. Here are two classic recipes; both of which are good stand-bys to be used with any combination of leaves or vegetables of your choice.

## CLASSIC VINAIGRETTE
Place 6 tablespoons olive oil, 2 tablespoons white wine vinegar or lemon juice, ½ teaspoon Dijon mustard and sea salt and freshly ground black pepper in a screw-topped jar and shake well to combine. Refrigerate and use as required.

## MAYONNAISE (makes 300ml/½ pt)
All the ingredients should be at room temperature to prevent the mayonnaise from curdling. Put 2 egg yolks, ½ teaspoon salt, 1 teaspoon Dijon mustard, freshly ground black pepper and 1 tablespoon of wine vinegar in a food processor. Blend until well combined. With the motor running, gradually trickle in 300ml (½ pt) olive oil, drop by drop to start with, then in a thin steady stream until all the oil has been added and you have smooth, thick mayonnaise. Add 1 more tablespoon of vinegar. Taste and adjust seasoning and store in a sealed container in the refrigerator for up to 2 weeks.

Lastly, salad making, like all cooking, should not be a chore! *Easy to Cook Salads* is a collection of salads that are quick and easy to prepare, yet also creative and tasty. Some, such as *Cajun Prawn Salad* and *Thai Beef Salad* have more involved preparation, but do not be put off trying them, because they, like all the recipes in this book, are described in easy steps, and the end result is well worth the effort.

Enjoy using this book and may it inspire you to experiment and to create your own, individual salads. Happy Salad Days!

# – 1 –
# CLASSIC FAVOURITES

# SALADE NIÇOISE

## INGREDIENTS

225 g (8 oz) French (green) beans
225 g (8 oz) new potatoes
200 g (7 oz) can tuna fish, drained
4 ripe tomatoes, quartered
4 hard-boiled eggs, quartered
8 anchovy fillets, halved and split
  lengthways
1 tablespoon capers, rinsed and
  drained
2 Little Gem lettuces, washed and
  separated into leaves
16 black olives
Dressing:
6 tablespoons extra virgin olive oil
2 tablespoons white wine vinegar
1 clove garlic, crushed
1 tablespoon Dijon mustard
½ teaspoon caster (superfine) sugar
1 tablespoon chopped fresh parsley
1 tablespoon chopped fresh basil

## METHOD

**Preparation time:** 30 minutes

Top and tail the French (green) beans and cook them in boiling water for 1 minute. Drain and set aside. Slice the potatoes thickly and cook in boiling, salted water until tender. Drain and allow to cool.

Whisk all the dressing ingredients together in a bowl until well combined. Season to taste. Flake the tuna into large chunks and place in a bowl with the beans, potatoes, tomatoes, eggs, anchovies and capers. Add the dressing and toss together gently.

Line a serving bowl with the lettuce leaves and pile the tuna mixture into the centre. Scattter over the black olives and serve at room temperature with crusty bread.

Serves 4

# CAESAR SALAD

## INGREDIENTS

1 cos (romaine) lettuce
150 ml (¼ pint/⅔ cup) virgin olive oil
2 thick slices white bread, crusts
   removed
4 anchovy fillets, drained, rinsed and
   dried
55 g (2 oz) Parmesan cheese
freshly ground black pepper
Dressing:
2 eggs
150 ml (¼ pint/⅔ cup) virgin olive oil
juice of 1 lemon
½ teaspoon Worcestershire sauce
1 clove garlic, crushed
sea salt and freshly ground black
   pepper

## METHOD

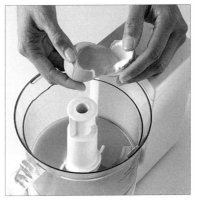

Wash the lettuce leaves and dry them in a salad spinner. Tear the leaves into large pieces and place them in a salad bowl. Heat the olive oil in a frying pan (skillet) until moderately hot. Cut the bread into small cubes and fry in the hot oil until crisp and golden. Remove with a slotted spoon and drain on paper towels. Chop the anchovies into tiny pieces.

Place the eggs in a pan of cold water, bring them to the boil, then reduce to a simmer and cook them for 2 minutes. Blend the remaining dressing ingredients together in a food processor until well combined. Break in the soft-boiled eggs and blend again until the dressing is creamy. Taste and adjust the seasoning if necessary.

Just before serving, use a swivel peeler to flake the Parmesan cheese. Pour the dressing over the lettuce leaves and sprinkle with the cheese flakes and anchovy pieces. Scatter over the croûtons and grind some black pepper over the salad. Toss at the table and serve at once.

NOTE:
The olive oil used to fry the croûtons can be strained into a bottle when cool and used to fry other food.

Serves 4

# WALDORF SALAD

## INGREDIENTS

*85 g (3 oz/¾ cup) walnut halves*
*6 sticks celery*
*4 red-skinned apples*
*1 tablespoon lemon juice*
*6 large radicchio leaves*
*Mayonnaise:*
*1 egg yolk*
*½ teaspoon Dijon mustard*
*¼ teaspoon salt*
*pinch of caster (superfine) sugar*
*freshly ground black pepper*
*150 ml (¼ pint/⅔ cup) grapeseed oil*
*1 tablespoon white wine vinegar*

## METHOD

Preparation time: 25 minutes

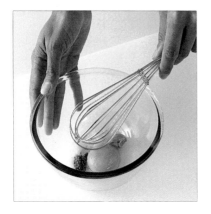

For the mayonnaise, place the egg yolk in a small bowl with the mustard, salt, sugar and pepper. Whisk together lightly until thoroughly combined. Start adding the oil drip by drip, whisking continuously until an emulsion is formed. When the mayonnaise begins to thicken, the oil may be added in a thin stream. Finally, blend in the vinegar, taste and adjust the seasoning if necessary.

Preheat the oven to 190°C (375°F/gas 5). Place the walnut halves on a baking sheet and bake them until they are toasted (about 10 minutes). Transfer to a plate and allow them to cool. Wash the celery, remove any stringy fibres and slice each stick thinly. Quarter and core the apples and cut them into neat chunks. Place the chunks in a small bowl and toss them in the lemon juice to prevent discoloration.

Wash and dry the radicchio leaves and tear them in half. Use them to line a large salad bowl. Place the celery, drained apple chunks and toasted walnuts in a separate bowl. Pour over the mayonnaise and toss well to combine. Spoon the mixture on to the salad leaves and serve at once.

NOTE:
If the mayonnaise curdles, gradually whisk in a tablespoon of hot water until the sauce is thick and shiny.

Serves 6–8

## INGREDIENTS

200 g (7 oz) feta cheese
4 tomatoes
½ cucumber
1 small onion, thinly sliced
8 calamata olives
8 large green olives
parsley and oregano sprigs to garnish
crusty sesame bread to serve
Dressing:
6 tablespoons virgin olive oil
2 tablespoons red wine vinegar
1 small clove garlic, crushed
1 tablespoon freshly chopped
    oregano
1 tablespoon freshly chopped parsley
sea salt and freshly ground black
    pepper
pinch of sugar

## METHOD

Preparation time: 15 minutes

Place all the dressing ingredients in a bowl and whisk well to combine. Adjust the seasoning if necessary and set aside.

Cut the feta cheese into cubes and place in a large salad bowl. Cut the tomatoes into wedges and add these to the bowl. Quarter the cucumber and slice it into chunks. Add these to the bowl along with the onions and olives.

Just before serving, pour the dressing over the salad and toss well to combine. Serve garnished with herb sprigs accompanied by warm sesame bread.

Serves 4

## INGREDIENTS

*½ large cucumber*
*1 teaspoon salt*
*½ lollo blondo lettuce, washed and*
*  separated into leaves*
*225 g (8 oz) ripe strawberries, hulled*
*  and sliced lengthways*
*Dressing:*
*2 teaspoons pink peppercorns in*
*  brine*
*3 tablespoons sunflower oil*
*1 tablespoon balsamic vinegar*
*salt and freshly ground black pepper*

---

METHOD                                    Preparation time: 25 minutes

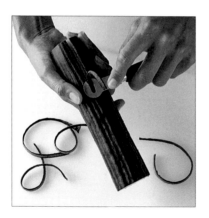

Using a canelle knife, remove strips of skin from the cucumber to create a ridged pattern. Slice it very thinly, then place on a plate and sprinkle with the salt. Leave it to stand for 15 minutes to draw out excess moisture.

Drain the peppercorns on paper towels. Place them in a bowl and crush coarsely with the back of a metal spoon. Add the oil and vinegar and whisk the dressing together until well combined. Season to taste. Rinse the sliced cucumber and dry it thoroughly on paper towels.

To serve, arrange the lettuce on four individual plates. Garnish with alternating circles of cucumber and strawberries. Spoon some dressing over each portion and serve at once.

Serves 4

## INGREDIENTS

*175 g (6 oz) orange cherry tomatoes*
*1 small purple onion*
*Dressing:*
*6 tablespoons extra virgin olive oil*
*2 tablespoons freshly squeezed lemon*
*   juice*
*salt and freshly ground black pepper*
*1 tablespoon chopped flat-leafed*
*   parsley*

## METHOD

Preparation time: 15 minutes

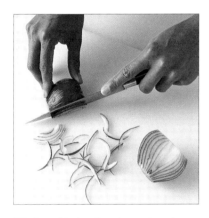

Wash and halve the cherry tomatoes and place them in a salad bowl. Peel the onion and cut into very thin strips and add these to the tomatoes.

Place all the dressing ingredients in a bowl and whisk well to combine. Season to taste.

About 10 minutes before serving, pour the dressing over the tomatoes and onions and mix well. Serve the salad at room temperature.

NOTE:
This salad can also be made with red cherry tomatoes if orange ones are unavailable.

Serves 4

*13*

## INGREDIENTS

*6 rashers (slices) streaky bacon*
*225 g (8 oz) hard French cheese*
*such as Comté or Cantal*
*4 tablespoons pine nuts*
*115 g (4 oz) Webbs lettuce*
*115 g (4 oz) oak leaf lettuce*
*Dressing:*
*1 teaspoon dark French mustard*
*¼ teaspoon salt*
*1 teaspoon caster (superfine) sugar*
*freshly ground black pepper*
*2 egg yolks, lightly beaten*
*2 tablespoons cider vinegar*
*3 tablespoons freshly chopped*
*parsley and thyme*
*4 tablespoons whipping cream*

## METHOD

**Preparation time:** 25 minutes

For the dressing, place the mustard, salt, sugar and pepper in a bowl. Gradually beat in the egg yolks and vinegar whisking well until they are thoroughly combined. Place the bowl over a pan of simmering water and cook, stirring occasionally, until the mixture thickens (about 4–5 minutes). Stir in the chopped herbs and chill thoroughly before folding in the cream just before serving.

Cook the rashers (slices) of bacon under a hot grill (broiler) for about 5 minutes on each side until they are crisp and golden. Leave to cool and then snip the bacon into strips. Cut the cheese into small cubes. Dry-fry the pine nuts in a pan, turning them constantly to prevent them from burning. When they are golden, tip them on to a plate and leave to cool. Separate the lettuces into leaves, wash and dry them.

To serve, tear the lettuce leaves into bite-sized pieces. Place them in a salad bowl and scatter over the bacon, cheese and pine nuts. Spoon over a little of the cream dressing and serve at once, passing extra dressing separately.

Serves 4

# BACON, LETTUCE AND TOMATO SALAD

## INGREDIENTS

6 rashers (slices) back bacon
2 slices granary bread
1 large clove garlic, peeled
150 ml (¼ pint/⅔ cup) olive oil
6 tomatoes
½ small iceberg lettuce, finely
  shredded
Dressing:
6 tablespoons olive oil
2 tablespoons sherry vinegar
2 tablespoons Blue Castello cheese
salt and freshly ground black pepper
pinch of paprika
pinch of sugar
2 tablespoons mayonnaise

## METHOD

Preparation time: 25 minutes

Cook the bacon under a preheated grill (broiler) until it is crisp and golden (about 10–15 minutes). Set it aside to cool. Cut the bread into small cubes. Halve the clove of garlic, then crush the halves slightly to bruise them. Place the garlic in a pan with the olive oil and heat the oil until it is moderately hot. Fry the bread cubes in batches until they are crisp, removing each batch with a slotted spoon and draining them on paper towels.

Wash the tomatoes and slice them into rings. Divide the shredded lettuce between four plates and arrange the tomato slices over the lettuce. Using scissors, snip the bacon into small pieces and scatter them over the lettuce and tomato.

Place all the dressing ingredients except the mayonnaise in a food processor. Blend together until it is smooth and creamy. Add the mayonnaise and blend together quickly. Taste and adjust the seasoning if necessary. Spoon a quarter of the dressing over each salad, sprinkle some croûtons over each portion and serve at once.

Serves 4

# Avocado, Scamorza and Tomato Salad

## INGREDIENTS

225 g (8 oz) Scamorza (smoked
  mozzarella cheese)
4 plum tomatoes
2 small avocados
2 teaspoons lemon juice
basil sprigs to garnish
warm ciabatta bread to serve
Vinaigrette:
6 tablespoons extra virgin olive oil
2 tablespoons red wine vinegar
6 large leaves of fresh basil
1 teaspoon Dijon mustard
2 tablespoons water
sea salt and freshly ground black
  pepper
pinch of sugar

## METHOD

Preparation time: 15 minutes

Slice the Scamorza as thinly as possible. Wash the tomatoes and cut them into several wedges. Peel and slice the avocados thinly. Place them on a plate and sprinkle with lemon juice to prevent discoloration.

Place all the dressing ingredients in a food processor. Blend for a couple of minutes until well combined. Taste and adjust the seasoning if necessary.

Divide the cheese, tomato wedges and sliced avocado between four plates. Drizzle over the basil vinaigrette, garnish each plate with a sprig of basil and serve at once with ciabatta bread.

NOTE:
If Scamorza is unavailable, substitute smoked Cheddar or Bavarian smoked cheese.

**Serves 4**

# – 2 –
# FRESH AND HEALTHY

# *Starfruit, Tofu and Frisée Salad*

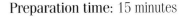

## INGREDIENTS

*225 g (8 oz) tofu (soya bean curd)*
*1 tablespoon sesame oil*
*½ head frisée lettuce*
*1 large starfruit*
*2 tablespoons toasted sunflower*
  *seeds*
*Dressing:*
*4 tablespoons sesame oil*
*3 tablespoons freshly squeezed*
  *orange juice*
*1 teaspoon clear honey*
*1 tablespoon white wine vinegar*
*salt and freshly ground black pepper*

## METHOD

**Preparation time:** 15 minutes

Cut the tofu into small cubes. Place the cubes on a baking sheet and sprinkle with the sesame oil. Cook under a preheated grill (broiler) for 5 minutes, turning the cubes over halfway through. Remove and set aside to cool.

Wash and dry the frisée lettuce, tear the leaves into bite-sized pieces and place in a salad bowl. Slice the starfruit thinly and add to the lettuce. Add the cooked tofu cubes to the bowl and set aside.

Place all the ingredients for the dressing in a screw-topped jar and shake well to combine. Taste and adjust the seasoning if necessary. Just before serving, pour the dressing over the salad and toss lightly to combine. Sprinkle over the sunflower seeds and serve immediately.

NOTE:
Smoked tofu can be used in this recipe to produce a stronger tasting salad.

Serves 4

# COTTAGE CHEESE AND PINEAPPLE SALAD

## INGREDIENTS

450 g (1 lb) low-fat cottage cheese
1 large red pepper (capsicum)
2 tablespoons freshly snipped chives
sea salt
1½ teaspoons tropical peppercorns
1 cos (romaine) lettuce
½ fresh pineapple
juice of 1 lime

## METHOD

Preparation time: 20 minutes

Place the cottage cheese in a mixing bowl. Halve the pepper and remove the core. Cut the pepper (capsicum) into small diamond shapes and add to the cottage cheese. Stir in the chives and some salt. Crush the peppercorns with a pestle and mortar and add to the cottage cheese. Mix well, taste and adjust the seasoning if necessary.

Discard any damaged, outer leaves from the lettuce. Wash and dry the remaining leaves and cut the larger leaves in half lengthways. Peel the pineapple, quarter it and remove the core. Cut each pineapple quarter lengthways into four pieces.

Divide the lettuce leaves between four serving plates and add 2 pieces of pineapple to each plate. Place a quarter of the cottage cheese in a neat mound on each plate. Sprinkle a little lime juice over the lettuce leaves and pineapple and serve immediately.

Serves 4

# ASPARAGUS, MANGETOUT AND YELLOW PEPPER SALAD

## INGREDIENTS

225 g (8 oz) asparagus, trimmed and
   cut into 5 cm (2 in) lengths
175 g (6 oz) mangetout (snow peas),
   topped and tailed
1 yellow pepper (capsicum)
Dressing:
4 tablespoons low-fat fromage frais
freshly squeezed juice of 1 lemon
freshly squeezed juice of 1 lime
2 tablespoons freshly snipped chives
sea salt and freshly ground black
   pepper
lemon and lime zest to garnish

METHOD                                                    Preparation time: 20 minutes

Blanch the asparagus in a pan of boiling, salted water for 2 minutes. Drain and refresh in cold water. Repeat the process with the mangetout (snow peas), blanching them for 1 minute. Halve the pepper (capsicum) and remove the seeds. Slice the flesh into long strips.

Remove a little zest from the lemon and lime using a zester. Cover and set aside for the garnish. Whisk together the dressing ingredients in a small bowl until thoroughly combined. Adjust the seasoning if necessary.

Place the prepared vegetables in a salad bowl. Pour over the dressing and toss to combine. Sprinkle with the citrus zest and serve immediately.

Serves 4

# LETTUCE, RADISH AND FRENCH BEAN SALAD

## INGREDIENTS

*200 g (7 oz) French (green) beans*
*4 Little Gem lettuces, each washed*
  *and cut into eight*
*12 radishes, washed and thinly sliced*
*1 tablespoon toasted sesame seeds*
*Dressing:*
*4 tablespoons sunflower oil*
*1 tablespoon sesame oil*
*1 tablespoon light tahini (sesame*
  *paste)*
*2 tablespoons white wine vinegar*
*salt and freshly ground black pepper*

## METHOD

Preparation time: 15 minutes

Place all the dressing ingredients in a bowl and whisk together until well combined. Taste, adjust the seasoning if necessary and set aside.

Top and tail the beans and cut them in half. Blanch them in a pan of boiling water for 2 minutes. Drain and refresh under cold water.

Place the lettuce, beans and radishes in a shallow serving bowl. Pour over the dressing, sprinkle with the toasted sesame seeds and serve immediately.

Serves 4–6

# GRAPEFRUIT, PRAWN AND FETA CHEESE SALAD

## INGREDIENTS

2 grapefruit
225 g (8 oz) cooked, peeled tiger
  prawns (shrimp)
200 g (7 oz) feta cheese, cubed
1 head red chicory (endive), washed
  and separated into leaves
1 head yellow chicory (endive),
  washed and separated into leaves
Dressing:
4 tablespoons light olive oil
2 tablespoons grapefruit juice
1 spring onion (scallion), thinly sliced
1 tablespoon freshly chopped parsley
salt and freshly ground black pepper

METHOD                                    Preparation time: 15 minutes

Peel the grapefruit with a small sharp knife and divide the flesh into segments, cutting in between the membrane. Do this over a bowl to save the grapefruit juice for the dressing.

Place the dressing ingredients in a screw-topped jar and shake well to combine. Adjust the seasoning if necessary. (Discard any remaining grapefruit juice.) Arrange the chicory (endive) leaves on a flat serving dish.

Place the prawns (shrimp), feta cheese and grapefruit segments in a salad bowl. Pour over the dressing and toss lightly to combine. Spoon this mixture over the chicory (endive) leaves and serve at once.

Serves 4

# MIXED LEAF SALAD WITH HAZELNUTS

## INGREDIENTS

*55 g (2 oz) skinless hazelnuts*
*225 g (8 oz) mixed salad leaves such*
  *as frisée, lollo rosso, oak leaf, cos*
  *(romaine), rocket (arugula),*
  *radicchio and lamb's lettuce (corn*
  *salad)*
*Dressing:*
*4 tablespoons hazelnut oil*
*1 tablespoon sunflower oil*
*4 teaspoons raspberry vinegar*
*salt and freshly ground black pepper*
*pinch of sugar*

## METHOD

Preparation time: 20 minutes

Preheat the oven to 190°C
(375°F/gas 5). Place the hazelnuts on
a baking sheet and cook them until
they are pale golden (about 10
minutes). Transfer them to a plate
and leave to cool.

Tear the larger salad leaves into bite-
sized pieces and keep the small ones
whole. Wash the leaves and dry them
in a salad spinner or between clean
tea towels (dish cloths). Transfer to a
serving bowl.

Halve the toasted hazelnuts and add
these to the bowl. Place the dressing
ingredients in a screw-topped jar and
shake thoroughly to combine. Taste
and adjust the seasoning if necessary
and pour the dressing over the salad
leaves. Toss lightly to combine and
serve immediately.

NOTE:
Try using walnuts and walnut oil
instead of hazelnuts and hazelnut oil
to vary the flavour of this salad.

Serves 4

# CARROT, CELERY, APPLE AND BRAZIL NUT SALAD

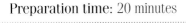

### INGREDIENTS

175 g (6 oz) carrots
175 g (6 oz) celery
1 large eating apple
2 teaspoons lemon juice
55 g (2 oz) brazil nuts
Dressing:
6 tablespoons grapeseed oil
2 tablespoons cider vinegar
3 tablespoons chopped mixed herbs
    such as parsley, chives, chervil and
    mint
salt and freshly ground black pepper

METHOD

Preparation time: 20 minutes

Cut the carrots into julienne strips. Wash the celery and slice it thinly on the diagonal. Cut the apple into quarters, core it and slice it very thinly. Sprinkle the lemon juice over the apple slices to prevent discoloration.

Place all the dressing ingredients in a screw-topped jar and shake well to combine thoroughly. Season to taste.

Place the carrots, celery, apple and brazil nuts in a large bowl. Pour over the dressing. Toss to combine and serve immediately.

Serves 4

# MELON, LIME AND MINT SALAD

## INGREDIENTS

1 ripe galia melon
2 pears
2 teaspoons lime juice
½ curly endive, washed and torn into
    small pieces
30 g (1 oz) lamb's lettuce (corn
    salad), washed
julienne strips of lime and mint
    sprigs to garnish
Dressing:
6 tablespoons grapeseed oil
3 tablespoons freshly squeezed lime
    juice
pinch of sea salt
½ teaspoon crushed dried green
    peppercorns
1 tablespoon freshly chopped mint

## METHOD

Preparation time: 25 minutes

Halve the melon and scoop out the
seeds. Using a melon baller, scoop out
the flesh into a bowl. Peel, core and
thinly slice the pears. Sprinkle with
lime juice to prevent discoloration.

Place the dressing ingredients in a
screw-topped jar and shake well to
combine. Adjust the seasoning if
necessary and set aside.

Place the curly endive and the lamb's
lettuce (corn salad) on a large platter.
Arrange the fruit on top and drizzle
over the dressing. Serve immediately
garnished with the lime julienne strips
and mint sprigs.

Serves 4

# FENNEL, SUGAR SNAP AND CUCUMBER SALAD

## INGREDIENTS

1 large head fennel
1 tablespoon lemon juice
115 g (4 oz) sugar snap peas, topped
  and tailed
½ large cucumber
12 black olives
12 green olives
Dressing:
6 tablespoons olive oil
2 tablespoons white wine vinegar
1 tablespoon dark French mustard
1 clove garlic, crushed
sea salt and freshly ground black
  pepper
pinch of sugar

## METHOD

**Preparation time:** 15 minutes

Remove the feathery fennel tops, chop them finely and add to the dressing ingredients in a small bowl. Whisk everything together to combine. Adjust the seasoning if necessary and set aside.

Slice the fennel thinly, then blanch it in boiling water with the lemon juice for 2 minutes. Drain and refresh under cold water. Blanch the sugar snap peas for 1 minute. Drain and refresh. Halve the cucumber lengthways, remove the seeds with a teaspoon and slice thickly.

Place the prepared vegetables and olives in a salad bowl. Pour over the dressing, toss well and serve immediately.

Serves 4

## INGREDIENTS

*85 g (3 oz) mixed herbs and salad
leaves per person, from the
following suggestions; flat-leafed
parsley, chervil, basil, chives and
flowers, nasturtium leaves and
flowers, sage and flowers, borage
flowers, marigold flowers, edible
pansy, sweet violet flowers, rocket
(arugula), sorrel, lamb's lettuce
(corn salad), lovage, endive, baby
spinach leaves*
*Dressing:*
*85 g (3 oz) watercress*
*1 clove garlic*
*1 tablespoon chopped shallot*
*2 tablespoons rice wine vinegar*
*5 tablespoons olive oil*
*salt and freshly ground black pepper*

## METHOD

Preparation time: 20 minutes

Wash the leaves and dry them between clean tea towels (dish cloths), taking care not to bruise them too much. Tear the leaves up into bite-sized pieces and place them in a salad bowl. Sprinkle any flowers you are using over the top and set the salad aside.

Wash the watercress and remove any thick stalks or roots. Place it in a food processor with the garlic, shallots, vinegar, oil, salt and pepper and blend in short bursts until everything is thoroughly combined and the dressing is smooth. Taste and adjust the seasoning if necessary.

Pour the dressing into a small bowl and serve the salad leaves separately, allowing people to dress their salads individually.

NOTE:
Fresh herbs will last for a few days if they are kept in well-sealed polythene bags in the refrigerator.

Serves 4–6

## INGREDIENTS

½ radicchio lettuce
½ lollo rosso lettuce
½ oak leaf lettuce
175 g (6 oz) button mushrooms
85 g (3 oz/¾ cup) pecan nuts
Dressing:
5 tablespoons light olive oil
3 tablespoons freshly squeezed lemon
  juice
3 tablespoons plain yoghurt
4 teaspoons freshly chopped thyme
1 teaspoon clear honey
salt and freshly ground black pepper

## METHOD

Preparation time: 25 minutes

Separate the lettuce leaves and break any large leaves into bite-sized pieces. Wash the pieces and dry them using a salad spinner or clean, dry tea towels (dish cloths). Place them in a large bowl and set aside.

Wipe the mushrooms clean and quarter them. Add them to the bowl of lettuce. Spread the pecan nuts out on a baking sheet and toast them under a moderately hot grill (broiler) for 5 minutes, turning them occasionally to prevent them from burning. Leave to cool while preparing the dressing.

Place all the dressing ingredients in a small bowl and whisk together until thoroughly combined. Taste and adjust the seasoning if necessary. Add the cooled pecan nuts to the lettuce and mushrooms, pour over the dressing, toss well and serve immediately.

Serves 6

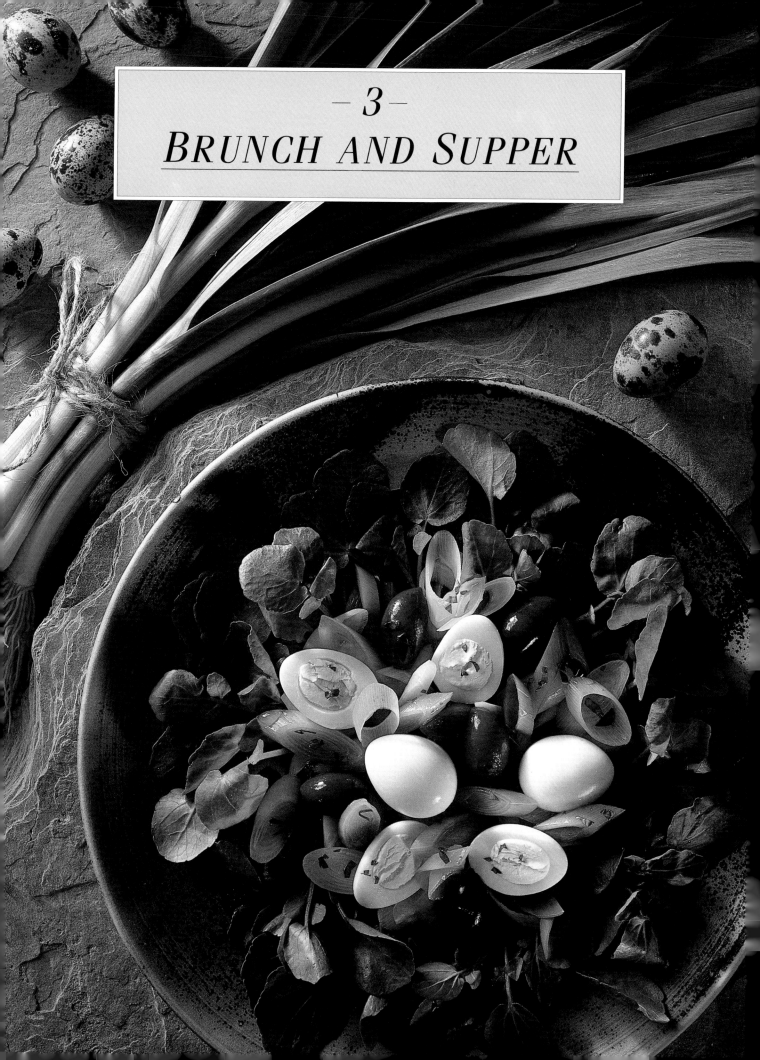

# - 3 -
# BRUNCH AND SUPPER

## INGREDIENTS

*2 red peppers (capsicums), halved and cored*
*2 orange peppers (capsicums), halved and cored*
*350 g (12 oz) Dolcelatte cheese, crumbled*
*225 g (8 oz) fresh rocket (arugula), washed*
*ciabatta bread to serve*
*Dressing:*
*2-3 tablespoons white wine vinegar*
*6 tablespoons extra virgin olive oil*
*1 clove garlic, crushed*
*1 teaspoon caster (superfine) sugar*
*1 tablespoon Dijon mustard*
*2 tablespoons freshly chopped chives*
*salt and freshly ground black pepper*

## METHOD

**Preparation time:** 20 minutes

Place the peppers (capsicums), skin side up, under a hot grill (broiler) and cook for 8–10 minutes until the skins begin to blacken. Remove them and cover with damp paper towels (this helps to loosen the skins, making them easier to peel). When cool enough to handle, skin the peppers and cut into neat strips.

Prepare the dressing by shaking all the ingredients together in a screw-topped jar. Season to taste.

To serve, place the rocket (arugula) in a shallow salad bowl, top with the pepper strips and crumbled cheese. Pour over the dressing, toss well and serve at once with hot ciabatta bread.

Serves 4

# BRESAOLA AND PALM HEART SALAD

## INGREDIENTS

400 g (14 oz) can palm hearts
1 small head chicory (endive)
½ lollo rosso lettuce
2 tablespoons pine nuts
12 thin slices Bresaola
Dressing:
6 tablespoons extra virgin olive oil
1½ tablespoons balsamic vinegar
1½ teaspoons Dijon mustard
2 teaspoons freshly chopped sage
salt and freshly ground black pepper
1 tablespoon water

## METHOD

Preparation time: 20 minutes

Drain the palm hearts and cut each piece into thick slices, on the diagonal. Divide the chicory (endive) into leaves and wash and dry it. Wash and dry the lollo rosso and break the leaves into large pieces.

Place all the dressing ingredients in a small bowl and whisk together until thoroughly combined. Taste and adjust the seasoning if necessary. Place the pine nuts on a baking sheet and cook under a preheated grill (broiler) for about 4 minutes, turning occasionally until they are toasted. Set aside to cool.

To serve, divide the salad leaves between four plates. Place three slices of Bresaola on each plate and divide the palm hearts between the four plates. Sprinkle over the pine nuts. Spoon some dressing over each portion and serve immediately.

NOTE:
Bresaola is cured beef. Italian salami could be substituted.

Serves 4

31

# AVOCADO, LABNA BALL AND CHERRY TOMATO SALAD

## INGREDIENTS

*450 g (1 lb) cherry tomatoes*
*15 labna balls in oil*
*2 avocados*
*1 Batavia lettuce*
*Dressing:*
*6 tablespoons extra virgin olive oil*
*2 tablespoons white wine vinegar*
*1 teaspoon finely chopped shallot*
*½ teaspoon Dijon mustard*
*sea salt and freshly ground black*
  *pepper*

## METHOD

Preparation time: 25 minutes

Place all the dressing ingredients in a screw-topped jar and shake well to combine. Taste and adjust the seasoning if necessary and set the dressing aside to allow the flavours to develop.

Wash and halve the cherry tomatoes. Drain the labna balls and halve them carefully, taking care not to break them up too much. Peel the avocados, remove the stones (pits) and slice the flesh thinly. Remove and discard any damaged outer leaves from the lettuce, wash and dry the remaining leaves and tear them into bite-sized pieces.

To serve, place the lettuce in a large salad bowl. Put the tomatoes, labna balls and avocado slices in a mixing bowl. Pour over the dressing and toss gently. Spoon this mixture on top of the lettuce leaves, grind over some black pepper and serve immediately.

NOTE:
Labna balls are Greek-style strained yoghurt balls and are available in Greek or Turkish delicatessens. If they are unavailable, try using individual mozzarella cheese balls.

Serves 6

# LEEK AND QUAIL'S EGG SALAD

## INGREDIENTS

450 g (1 lb) young leeks
16 quail's eggs
1 bunch watercress
20 Calamata olives
Vinaigrette:
6 tablespoons light olive oil
1½ tablespoons balsamic vinegar
2 tablespoons chopped flat-leafed
   parsley
sea salt and freshly ground black
   pepper

## METHOD

Preparation time: 30 minutes

Wash and trim the leeks and slice them fairly thinly, on the diagonal. Cook them in boiling, salted water for 3–4 minutes until just tender. Drain and refresh them under cold water and set aside.

Place the quail's eggs in a pan of cold water and bring them to the boil. Reduce the heat to a simmer and cook the eggs for 3 minutes. Plunge them into cold water and when they are cool enough to handle, peel them. Trim the tough stalks from the watercress and wash and dry the leaves.

Place the vinaigrette ingredients in a screw-topped jar and shake well to combine. Taste and adjust the seasoning if necessary. To serve, divide the watercress between four plates. Place the leeks and olives in a bowl and pour over the dressing, toss to combine and divide the mixture between the four plates. Halve 8 of the eggs and place 2 whole eggs and 4 halves on each plate. Serve immediately.

Serves 4

# GRILLED GOAT'S CHEESE SALAD

## INGREDIENTS

*225 g (8 oz) mixed radicchio lettuce*
  *and lamb's lettuce (corn salad)*
*generous handful of Italian parsley*
  *leaves*
*8 slices French bread*
*2 tablespoons extra virgin olive oil*
*225 g (8 oz) soft goat's cheese*
*freshly ground black pepper*
*Dressing:*
*6 tablespoons virgin olive oil*
*2 tablespoons white wine vinegar*
*2 tablespoons dark French mustard*
*3 cloves garlic, crushed*
*¼ teaspoon caster (superfine) sugar*
*salt and freshly ground black pepper*

## METHOD

Preparation time: 20 minutes

Whisk the dressing ingredients together until thoroughly combined. Taste and adjust the seasoning if necessary and set aside. Tear the radicchio leaves into bite-sized pieces. Wash the salad and parsley leaves and dry them in a salad spinner. Transfer to a mixing bowl and set aside.

Brush one side of each piece of bread lightly with olive oil and toast them under a moderately hot grill (broiler) until lightly golden. Remove from the grill and slice or spread the goat's cheese on to the untoasted sides of the bread. Grind over some black pepper and cook under a moderate grill for a few more minutes until the cheese melts.

To serve, pour the dressing over the salad leaves and toss well. Divide the salad between four plates. top each plate with 2 slices of freshly grilled goat's cheese bread and serve immediately.

Serves 4

# WARM MUSHROOM AND PECORINO SALAD

## INGREDIENTS

*350 g (12 oz) mixed mushrooms,*
  *such as brown cap, oyster, shitake,*
  *chantarelles, ceps, field and girolle*
*6 tablespoons extra virgin olive oil*
*55 g (2 oz) rocket (arugula)*
*115 g (4 oz) Pecorino cheese*
*1 tablespoon lemon juice*
*sea salt and freshly ground black*
  *pepper*
*crusty bread to serve*

## METHOD

Preparation time: 20 minutes

Wipe the mushrooms and slice any large ones. Heat 2 tablespoons of the oil in a large frying pan (skillet) and sauté half the mushrooms for 1 minute, stirring constantly. Season them with salt and pepper and tip them into a bowl. Cook the remaining mushrooms in the same way with 2 more tablespoons of the oil.

Wash and dry the rocket (arugula) and place it in a shallow serving bowl. Use a swivel peeler and pare the Pecorino cheese into thin slivers. Set it aside.

Whisk together the remaining olive oil and the lemon juice with some salt and pepper and drizzle this over the rocket. Spoon the sautéed mushrooms into the centre, sprinkle over the Pecorino cheese and serve immediately, with warm crusty bread.

Serves 4

# PARMA HAM, FIG AND ARTICHOKE SALAD

## INGREDIENTS

*175 g (6 oz) mixed salad leaves*
*4 ripe figs*
*8 artichoke hearts in oil, drained*
*4 tablespoons virgin olive oil*
*1 tablespoon balsamic vinegar*
*sea salt and freshly ground black*
  *pepper*
*8 large slices Parma ham*
  *(prosciutto)*

METHOD                                    Preparation time: 20 minutes

Tear the larger salad leaves into bite-sized pieces. Wash and dry them using a salad spinner or clean tea towels (dish cloths). Set them aside.

Peel the skin off the figs using a small sharp knife. Cut each fig into quarters, cutting almost through to the base so each fig remains intact. Halve the artichoke hearts. Place 3 tablespoons of the olive oil and the balsamic vinegar in a screw-topped jar and shake well to combine. Season lightly with salt and pepper and set aside.

To serve, toss the lettuce leaves lightly in the dressing and divide them between four plates. Place 2 slices of ham, 1 fig and 4 artichoke halves on each plate. Drizzle the remaining tablespoon of olive oil lightly over each portion. Grind over some black pepper and serve immediately.

**Serves 4**

# WARM CHICKEN LIVER, SAGE AND ORANGE SALAD

## INGREDIENTS

225 g (8 oz) mixed green salad
   leaves, such as lollo blondo, frisée
   and escarole lettuces
2 large oranges
450 g (1 lb) chicken livers
salt and freshly ground black pepper
55 g (2 oz/¼ cup) unsalted butter
2 tablespoons freshly chopped sage
*Dressing:*
4 tablespoons sunflower oil
2 tablespoons reserved orange juice
1 teaspoon grated orange zest
1 teaspoon Dijon mustard
sea salt and freshly ground black
   pepper

## METHOD

Preparation time: 25 minutes

Tear the lettuce leaves into bite-sized pieces and wash and dry them. Place them in a shallow serving bowl and set aside. Grate 1 teaspoon of orange zest for the dressing; then peel the oranges and using a small sharp knife, cut in between the membranes to divide the flesh into segments. Do this over a bowl to collect the orange juice for the dressing.

Trim and slice the livers. Rinse them and pat them dry on paper towels. Season well with salt and pepper. Melt the butter in a large frying pan (skillet) and when it begins to foam, add the livers and chopped sage. Cook over a medium heat, stirring occasionally until the livers are just cooked through (about 5 minutes).

Place the dressing ingredients in a screw-topped jar and shake well to combine. Taste and adjust the seasoning if necessary. To serve, spoon the warm chicken livers and the orange segments over the lettuce leaves, pour over the dressing and serve immediately.

Serves 4

# SMOKED CHICKEN AND SUN-DRIED TOMATO SALAD

## INGREDIENTS

350 g (12 oz) smoked chicken
5 halves of sun-dried tomatoes in oil
3 sticks celery
16 green olives
½ Batavia lettuce
Dressing:
2 tablespoons sunflower oil
2 tablespoons olive oil
1 teaspoon coarse-grain mustard
1 tablespoon red wine vinegar
1 clove garlic, crushed
sea salt and freshly ground black
  pepper
pinch of sugar

## METHOD

**Preparation time: 25 minutes**

Remove the skin from the smoked chicken and cut the flesh into neat, bite-sized pieces. Slice the sun-dried tomatoes into thin strips. Wash the celery and slice thinly on the diagonal.

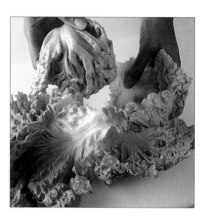

Put all the dressing ingredients in a small bowl and whisk them together until thoroughly combined. Taste and adjust the seasoning if necessary. Separate the lettuce into leaves and wash and dry them.

To serve, line a shallow bowl with the lettuce leaves. Place the chicken, sun-dried tomatoes, celery and green olives in a mixing bowl. Pour over the dressing and toss well to combine. Spoon the chicken mixture into the centre of the salad leaves and serve at once.

Serves 4

# SMOKED SALMON AND NEW POTATO SALAD

## INGREDIENTS

*20 baby new potatoes*
*175 g (6 oz) smoked salmon*
*2 Little Gem lettuces*
*1 tablespoon capers*
*Dressing:*
*3 tablespoons cream cheese*
*1½ tablespoons lemon juice*
*6 tablespoons sunflower oil*
*4 teaspoons freshly snipped chives*
*sea salt and freshly ground black*
  *pepper*
*pinch of sugar*

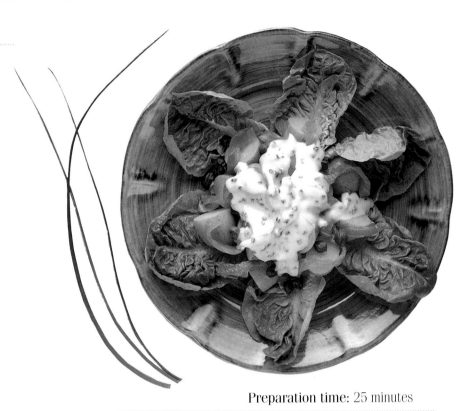

## METHOD

Preparation time: 25 minutes

Scrub the potatoes and halve them. Bring a pan of salted water to the boil and cook the potatoes until they are tender (about 8–10 minutes). Drain, refresh them under cold water and set aside. Slice the salmon into thin strips and set it aside.

Place all the dressing ingredients except the chives in a food processor and blend until well combined. Add the chives and blend again for a few seconds. Taste and adjust the seasoning if necessary.

Separate the lettuce leaves, wash and dry them and then use them to line a shallow bowl. Pile the potatoes and salmon into the centre. Sprinkle over the capers and pour over the dressing. Serve immediately.

Serves 4

## INGREDIENTS

*175 g (6 oz) Stilton cheese*
*1 tablespoon walnut oil*
*55 g (2 oz/½ cup) walnut pieces*
*pinch of sea salt*
*12 large radicchio leaves*
*3 small pears, quartered and cored*
*2 tablespoons lemon juice*
*Dressing:*
*1 tablespoon walnut oil*
*2 tablespoons sunflower oil*
*1 tablespoon red wine vinegar*
*sea salt and freshly ground black*
*  pepper*
*¼ teaspoon caster (superfine) sugar*

## METHOD

**Preparation time:** 25 minutes

Remove the rind from the Stilton and crumble the cheese into small cubes. Heat the walnut oil in a small pan and cook the walnut pieces over a medium heat for 2-3 minutes. Remove with a slotted spoon, drain on paper towels and sprinkle with sea salt. Wash and dry the radicchio leaves.

Slice the pears thinly and toss them in a shallow bowl with the lemon juice to prevent them discolouring. Place the ingredients for the dressing in a small bowl and whisk together until thoroughly combined. Taste and adjust the seasoning if necessary.

To serve, tear the lettuce leaves into quarters and divide them between four plates. Drain the lemon juice from the pears and add the Stilton and walnuts to the bowl. Pour over the dressing and toss well to combine. Divide the pear, cheese and nut mixture between the four plates and serve immediately.

Serves 4

# SPINACH, EGG AND SMOKED HAM SALAD

## INGREDIENTS

*225 g (8 oz) baby spinach leaves*
*175 g (6 oz) smoked ham*
*4 eggs*
*3 slices white bread, crusts removed*
*olive oil for frying*
*Vinaigrette:*
*4 tablespoons olive oil*
*1 tablespoon cider vinegar*
*1 tablespoon mayonnaise*
*1 teaspoon coarse-grain mustard*
*1 large clove garlic, crushed*
*salt and freshly ground black pepper*

## METHOD

Preparation time: 25 minutes

Wash and dry the spinach leaves and place them in a large bowl. Slice the ham into thin strips and add these to the spinach. Place the eggs in a pan of cold water, bring the water to the boil and boil the eggs for 7–8 minutes to hard-boil them. Run under cold water until they are cool enough to handle, then peel off the shells.

Cut the bread into 1.25 cm (½ in) squares. Pour enough olive oil into a pan to fill it to a depth of 1.25 cm (½ in), heat and then fry the bread in batches until golden. Drain the croûtons on paper towels to remove excess oil.

Place the dressing ingredients in a screw-topped jar and shake well to combine. Taste and adjust the seasoning if necessary. To serve, pour the dressing over the spinach and ham, toss gently to combine and divide the salad between four plates. Quarter the eggs and place an egg on each plate. Divide the croûtons between the plates and serve immediately.

Serves 4

# TUNA AND TOMATO SALAD CUPS

INGREDIENTS

4 ripe beef tomatoes
200 g (7 oz) can tuna chunks in brine
½ cucumber, cut into small cubes
12 pitted black olives, sliced
2 tablespoons freshly snipped chives
8 tablespoons plain yoghurt
salt and freshly ground black pepper
½ iceberg lettuce
3 tablespoons light olive oil
1 tablespoon lemon juice
rye bread to serve

METHOD                                    Preparation time: 30 minutes

Slice the tops off the tomatoes and reserve them. Using a teaspoon, scoop out the seeds and flesh from the tomatoes and discard. Sprinkle a little salt into each tomato shell and turn upside down on paper towels to drain while preparing the other ingredients.

Drain the tuna and flake it into small chunks. Place it in a mixing bowl with the cucumber, olives, chives and yoghurt. Season the mixture well with salt and pepper and toss gently until everything is well-coated in yoghurt. Taste and adjust the seasoning if necessary.

Shred the lettuce and place it in a mixing bowl. Whisk together the oil, lemon juice and some salt and pepper and pour this over the lettuce. Toss lightly to combine and divide the lettuce between four serving plates. Spoon a quarter of the tuna mixture into each tomato, replace the lids at an angle and place a tomato on each plate of lettuce. Serve immediately with rye bread.

Serves 4

# WHEAT BERRY SALAD WITH SUNFLOWER SEEDS

## INGREDIENTS

225 g (8 oz) wheat berries
4 tablespoons sunflower seeds
1 bunch spring onions (scallions)
2 bunches watercress
3 tablespoons freshly chopped basil
3 tablespoons freshly chopped dill
Dressing:
6 tablespoons grapeseed oil
2 tablespoons balsamic vinegar
1 tablespoon coarse grain mustard
sea salt and freshly ground black
  pepper

METHOD                                    Preparation time: 15 minutes

Soak the wheat berries in cold water overnight. Place the wheat berries in a pan of fresh water, bring to the boil and simmer for about 1 hour until they are tender but still retain a chewy texture. Some of the berries will pop open to reveal the white grain inside.

Place the sunflower seeds in a frying pan (skillet) and dry-fry them for a couple of minutes, turning frequently to prevent them from burning. Set them aside to cool. Wash and trim the spring onions and slice them thinly. Place the dressing ingredients in a screw-topped jar and shake well to combine. Taste and adjust the seasoning if necessary and set it aside.

Discard any tough stalks from the watercress and wash and dry it. Use it to line a shallow serving bowl. Place the wheat berries, sunflower seeds, spring onions (scallions) and chopped herbs in a mixing bowl. Pour over the dressing and toss well to combine. Taste and adjust the seasoning if necessary. Spoon this mixture on to the bed of watercress and serve at once.

Serves 6

## INGREDIENTS

55 g (2 oz/¼ cup) wild rice
175 g (6 oz/¾ cup) long-grain rice
2 skinned, boned chicken breasts
2 tablespoons groundnut oil
175 g (6 oz) dwarf beans
1 red pepper (capsicum)
4 tablespoons coarsely chopped
  tarragon
55 g (2 oz/½ cup) salted cashew
  nuts
Dressing:
½ teaspoon green peppercorns in
  brine
6 tablespoons groundnut oil
2 tablespoons tarragon vinegar
2 teaspoons Dijon mustard
sea salt and freshly ground black
  pepper
pinch of sugar

## METHOD

Preparation time: 30 minutes

Cook the wild rice in boiling, salted water for 30–35 minutes until it is tender. Drain and refresh it under cold water and set it aside. Cook the long-grain rice in boiling, salted water for 8–10 minutes until cooked. Drain and refresh it, then set aside.

Slice the chicken into strips and season it well. Fry it with the groundnut oil for 4–5 minutes until golden and cooked through. Set it aside to cool. Top and tail the beans and cut them into 2.5 cm (1 in) pieces. Cook them in boiling, salted water for 2 minutes. Drain and refresh them. Halve the pepper (capsicum) and remove the core and seeds and chop the pepper into large dice. Place all the prepared ingredients in a bowl and add the tarragon and cashew nuts.

Chop the peppercorns finely and place all the dressing ingredients in a screw-topped jar. Shake well to combine. Pour the dressing over the salad ingredients and toss well. Taste and adjust the seasoning if necessary and serve at once.

Serves 6

# THREE BEAN SALAD

### INGREDIENTS

*430 g (15 oz) can red kidney beans*
*430 g (15 oz) can black eye beans*
*225 g (8 oz) can butter beans*
*3 sticks celery*
*5 spring onions (scallions)*
*Dressing:*
*6 tablespoons sunolive oil*
*1½ tablespoons white wine vinegar*
*4 tablespoons freshly chopped*
  *coriander (cilantro)*
*salt and freshly ground black pepper*

## METHOD

Preparation time: 15 minutes

Rinse the beans under cold running water and then set them aside in a colander to drain. Wash the celery and remove any stringy fibres with a small, sharp knife. Cut the celery on the diagonal into 5 mm (¼ in) slices.

Wash and dry the spring onions (scallions) and cut both the white and green parts into 5 mm (¼ in) slices. Place all the dressing ingredients in a small bowl and whisk together to form an emulsion. Taste and adjust the seasoning if necessary.

Place the beans, celery and spring onions in a large salad bowl. Pour over the dressing and toss to combine thoroughly. If time permits, leave the salad to stand for about an hour before serving to allow the flavours to develop.

**Serves 6**

# BORLOTTI BEAN, AVOCADO AND GRUYÈRE SALAD

## INGREDIENTS

*2 x 430 g (15 oz) cans borlotti beans*
*115 g (4 oz/1 cup) Gruyère cheese*
*1 large or 2 small avocados*
*1 tablespoon lemon juice*
*Dressing:*
*6 tablespoons rapeseed oil*
*2 ½ tablespoons white wine vinegar*
*2 teaspoons Dijon mustard*
*1 egg yolk*
*¼ teaspoon paprika*
*sea salt and freshly ground black*
  *pepper*
*pinch of sugar*

## METHOD

Preparation time: 20 minutes

Place the borlotti beans in a colander and rinse them thoroughly under cold water. Drain and transfer them to a large salad bowl. Grate the cheese coarsely and add this to the bowl of beans.

Peel and halve the avocado, remove the stone (pit) and dice the flesh into neat chunks. Toss the chunks with the lemon juice in a small bowl to prevent discoloration. Place all the dressing ingredients in a food processor and blend until thoroughly combined and a smooth dressing is produced. Taste and adjust the seasoning, adding more paprika if it is not spicy enough.

To serve, drain the avocado chunks and add them to the bowl of beans and cheese. Season well with salt and pepper. Pour over the creamy paprika dressing, toss gently to combine and serve immediately.

Serves 6–8

# SPICY PASTA AND EGG SALAD

### INGREDIENTS

225 g (8 oz) dried penne pasta
2 eggs
8 tablespoons extra virgin olive oil
3 cloves garlic
4 shallots
1 large red chilli
4 tablespoons freshly chopped
  coriander (cilantro)
2 tablespoons capers
1 tablespoon white wine vinegar
sea salt and freshly ground black
  pepper
8 black olives
8 green olives

### METHOD

Preparation time: 30 minutes

Place a few drops of oil in a pan of boiling, salted water and cook the penne for about 10 minutes. Drain and refresh under cold water, then set aside. Cook the eggs in a pan of boiling water for 10 minutes to hard boil them. Drain and plunge them into cold water until they are cool enough to handle, then peel them.

Peel the garlic and slice it into thin slivers. Peel the shallots and slice them thinly. Deseed and slice the chilli. Heat 2 tablespoons of the oil in a frying pan (skillet) and cook the garlic, shallots and chilli for 5-6 minutes until crisp and golden. Remove with a slotted spoon and drain on paper towels.

Place the remaining oil, chopped coriander (cilantro), capers, vinegar and seasoning in a screw-topped jar and shake well until thoroughly combined. To serve, place the pasta and olives in a salad bowl. Pour over the dressing and toss well to combine. Quarter the eggs and arrange them on top of the salad. Sprinkle with the fried shallot mixture and serve immediately.

Serves 4

# ROQUEFORT AND PASTA SALAD

## INGREDIENTS

1 tablespoon vegetable oil
6 rashers (slices) streaky bacon
1 red pepper (capsicum)
175 g (6 oz) pasta shapes
175 g (6 oz) Roquefort cheese,
  broken into cubes
*Vinaigrette:*
6 tablespoons olive oil
2 tablespoons red wine vinegar
1 clove garlic, crushed
2 tablespoons snipped chives
1 teaspoon Dijon mustard
salt and freshly ground black pepper

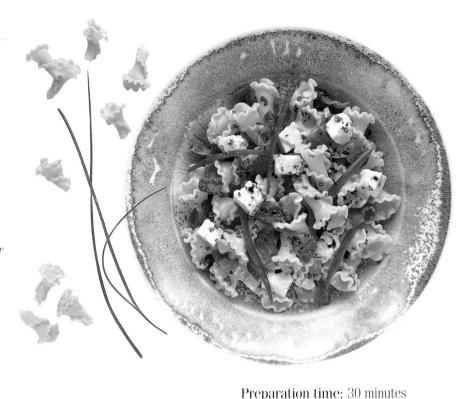

## METHOD

Preparation time: 30 minutes

Heat the oil in a large frying pan (skillet) and cook the bacon rashers (slices), turning them once until they are golden (about 5 minutes). When they are cool enough to handle, cut them into thick strips using scissors.

Halve the pepper (capsicum) and remove the seeds and core. Slice the pepper into long, thin strips. Place the vinaigrette ingredients in a screw-topped jar and shake well until thoroughly combined. Taste and adjust the seasoning if necessary.

Cook the pasta for 8–10 minutes in a pan of boiling, salted water to which a few drops of oil have been added. (This will prevent the pasta from sticking.) When cooked *al dente* drain the pasta and tip it into a large salad bowl. Add the bacon, cheese and pepper to the bowl, pour over the dressing and toss to combine. Serve immediately while the pasta is still warm.

Serves 4–6

# ORECCHIETTE, BROCCOLI AND PINE NUT SALAD

## INGREDIENTS

*175 g (6 oz) orecchiette pasta*
*450 g (1 lb) broccoli*
*4 tablespoons pine nuts*
*Dressing:*
*6 tomatoes*
*3 anchovy fillets, finely chopped*
*4 tablespoons white wine vinegar*
*6 tablespoons virgin olive oil*
*freshly ground black pepper*

METHOD                                    Preparation time: 30 minutes

Cook the pasta for 10 minutes in a pan of boiling, salted water to which a few drops of oil have been added to prevent the pasta from sticking. Drain and refresh the pasta under cold water and set it aside. Divide the broccoli into florets and cook it in a pan of boiling, salted water for 3–4 minutes. Drain and refresh it under cold water.

Place the pine nuts on a baking sheet and cook them under a hot grill (broiler) for a few minutes until golden, turning them frequently to prevent burning. Set them aside to cool. Peel and deseed the tomatoes and place them in a food processor with the remaining dressing ingredients. Blend to a thick, smooth dressing. Taste and adjust the seasoning if necessary.

Place the pasta, broccoli and pine nuts in a salad bowl. Pour over the dressing and toss well. If time permits, refrigerate the salad for about an hour to allow the flavours to develop.

NOTE:
To remove tomato skins easily, cut a cross at the base of each tomato, place them in a bowl and cover with boiling water. When the skins begin to 'pop' remove the tomatoes from the water, cool and peel.

Serves 4–6

# BROAD BEAN SALAD

## INGREDIENTS

*450 g (1 lb) frozen broad (fava)*
*  beans*
*12 dried apricots*
*55 g (2 oz/½ cup) blanched almonds*
*2 orange peppers (capsicums)*
*12 slices Italian salami*
*Dressing:*
*6 tablespoons virgin olive oil*
*2 tablespoons cider vinegar*
*2 teaspoons coarse-grain mustard*
*sea salt and freshly ground black*
*  pepper*
*pinch of sugar*

## METHOD

Preparation time: 25 minutes

Cook the broad (fava) beans in a pan of boiling, salted water until they are tender (about 5–6 minutes). Drain and refresh them under cold water. Slice the apricots into thin strips and place them in a large salad bowl with the drained beans.

Place the almonds on a baking sheet and toast them under a hot grill (broiler) for 3–4 minutes until they are golden. Leave to cool and then add them to the bowl. Halve and core the peppers (capsicums) and chop them into large dice. Chop the salami into long strips. Add the peppers and salami to the bowl.

Place the ingredients for the dressing in a small bowl and whisk them together until thoroughly combined. Taste and adjust the seasoning if necessary. Pour the dressing over the salad ingredients and toss well to combine. If time permits, leave the salad to stand for an hour before serving to allow the flavours to develop.

Serves 6

51

# COUS COUS AND MEDITERRANEAN VEGETABLE SALAD

## INGREDIENTS

*225 g (8 oz) cous cous*
*1 medium aubergine (eggplant),*
  *about 225 g (8 oz)*
*115 g (4 oz) courgettes (zucchini)*
*1 orange pepper (capsicum)*
*1 yellow pepper (capsicum)*
*2 tablespoons olive oil*
*2 tablespoons pine nuts*
*1 purple onion*
*2 tablespoons raisins*
*Dressing:*
*2 teaspoons lime zest*
*1 tablespoon fresh lime juice*
*2 tablespoons chopped flat-leafed*
  *parsley*
*1 clove garlic*
*3 tablespoons virgin olive oil*
*sea salt*
*pinch of sugar*
*¼-½ teaspoon harissa paste*

## METHOD

**Preparation time:** 30 minutes

Place the cous cous in a bowl and just cover with boiling water. Leave to stand for about 10 minutes to allow the grains to swell. When all the water has been absorbed, separate the grains using your fingers and set aside.

Halve the aubergine (eggplant), courgettes (zucchini) and peppers (capsicums) lengthways, remove the cores from the peppers and use 1 tablespoon of the oil to brush the vegetables all over. Lay them skin-side up on a grill rack (broiler) and cook until the skins are charred and the vegetables are cooked (about 10 minutes on each side).

Cool the grilled vegetables and remove the skins from the peppers, then dice all the vegetables into neat chunks and set aside.

Peel the onion and chop it finely. Place the remaining tablespoon of olive oil in a small pan and cook the pine nuts for about 1 minute until they are golden. Remove with a slotted spoon and drain on paper towels.

Grate 2 teaspoons of lime zest and then squeeze the juice from the lime. Crush the garlic. Place all the dressing ingredients in a screw-topped jar and shake well to combine. Taste and adjust the seasoning and the amount of harissa paste, if liked.

Place all the ingredients in a large serving bowl, pour over the dressing, taste and adjust the seasoning if necessary and serve immediately.

Serves 4-6

NOTE:

Harissa is a hot North African chilli paste which can be bought from speciality shops. If it is unavailable, hot chilli sauce is an alternative.

*Grilling these vegetables brings out all their natural flavours, enhancing them with a robust chargrilled taste. Other vegetables that are delicious when cooked this way are onions, plum tomatoes, fennel and chicory.*

# TABBOULEH SALAD

## INGREDIENTS

175 g (6 oz) bulghar wheat
2 cloves garlic, finely chopped
4 tablespoons extra virgin olive oil
juice of 1½ lemons
sea salt and freshly ground black
  pepper
30 g (1 oz) flat-leafed parsley leaves
30 g (1 oz) mint leaves
4 spring onions (scallions)
1 large plum tomato
½ cucumber
cos (romaine) lettuce leaves, parsley
  and mint sprigs to garnish

## METHOD

Preparation time: 30 minutes

Place the bulghar wheat in a bowl and just cover it with boiling water. Set it aside for 20–30 minutes for the grains to swell and then drain it thoroughly. Place the bulghar wheat in a clean tea-towel (dish cloth) and squeeze to remove excess moisture. Transfer to a large bowl.

Mix together the garlic, olive oil, lemon juice, salt and pepper. Pour the oily dressing over the bulghar, stir it well and allow it to stand while preparing the other ingredients.

Coarsely chop the parsley and mint, thinly slice the spring onions (scallions) and dice the tomato into small chunks. Peel and dice the cucumber. Add the prepared herbs and vegetables to the bulghar. Stir well and adjust the seasoning if necessary. Transfer the tabbouleh to a serving dish and serve garnished with cos (romaine) lettuce leaves and herb sprigs.

Serves 4

# Chick Pea and Chorizo Sausage Salad

## INGREDIENTS

175 g (6 oz) raw chorizo sausage
1 tablespoon vegetable oil
430 g (15 oz) can chick peas
  (garbanzo beans)
½ small onion
1 green pepper (capsicum)
Vinaigrette:
4 tablespoons light olive oil
1 tablespoon sherry vinegar
2 tablespoons freshly chopped
  parsley
sea salt and freshly ground black
  pepper
pinch of sugar

## METHOD

Preparation time: 20 minutes

Slice the chorizo sausage and fry it with the vegetable oil for about 2 minutes until it is cooked. Remove it with a slotted spoon and drain on paper towels. Rinse the chick peas (garbanzo beans) in a colander and drain them.

Slice the onion thinly. Halve the pepper (capsicum) and remove the seeds and core. Cut it into diamond-shaped pieces. Place the vinaigrette ingredients in a screw-topped jar and shake well to combine. Taste and adjust the seasoning if necessary.

Place the chorizo, chick peas, onion and pepper on a serving plate. Pour over the dressing and toss well to combine. If time permits, let the salad stand for 1 hour before serving to allow the flavours to develop.

Serves 6

# CELERIAC, BLACK BEAN AND FLAGEOLET SALAD

### INGREDIENTS

115 g (4 oz) dried black kidney beans
115 g (4 oz) dried flageolet beans
225 g (8 oz) celeriac
1 purple onion
Vinaigrette:
3 tablespoons sunflower oil
2 tablespoons red wine vinegar
2 tablespoons soured cream
2 tablespoons freshly chopped thyme
½ teaspoon English mustard
sea salt and freshly ground black
  pepper

---

METHOD                                    Preparation time: 20 minutes

Soak the beans in separate bowls of cold water overnight, then rinse them and cook them in pans of boiling salted water until they are tender, boiling rapidly for the first 10 minutes. The flageolet beans will take about 40 minutes and the black beans will cook for 1–1¼ hours. Drain the cooked beans and refresh them in cold water, then transfer them to a large bowl and set aside.

Peel the celeriac and cut it into 2.5 cm (1 in) cubes. Cook the celeriac in boiling, salted water until it is tender (about 5-6 minutes). Drain and refresh it and add it to the bowl of beans.

Peel the onion and slice it into thin rings. Add these to the bowl of ingredients. Place all the vinaigrette ingredients in a screw-topped jar and shake well to combine. Taste and adjust the seasoning if necessary and pour over the beans and celeriac. Toss well to combine and if time permits, refrigerate the salad for 1 hour before serving to allow the flavours to develop.

Serves 6

# – 5 –
# SPICY AND EXOTIC

### INGREDIENTS

*16 large king scallops*
*sea salt and freshly ground black*
*  pepper*
*2 tablespoons groundnut oil*
*1½ tablespoons finely chopped fresh*
*  ginger root*
*1 green chilli, seeded and chopped*
*3 tablespoons fresh lime juice*
*225 g (8 oz) soft lettuce leaves, such*
*  as lollo blondo, monet and round*
*  lettuce*
*julienne of lime to garnish*
*Dressing:*
*6 tablespoons groundnut oil*
*3 tablespoons rice wine vinegar*
*4 tablespoons freshly chopped*
*  coriander (cilantro)*
*sea salt and freshly ground black*
*  pepper*

### METHOD

**Preparation time: 25 minutes**

Pare some strips of lime zest from the lime and set aside. Separate the corals from the white part of the scallops and halve any large whites. Season well. Heat the oil in a large pan. Add the ginger and chilli and cook for a few seconds, then add the white part of the scallops and cook for about 2 minutes. Add the corals and lime juice and cook for a further 1–2 minutes. Transfer the contents of the pan to a plate and leave to cool.

Wash and dry the lettuce leaves and tear them into bite-sized pieces. Place them in a large bowl. Cut fine julienne strips from the reserved lime zest and blanch it for 30 seconds in boiling water. Drain and refresh it in cold water and set aside.

Place the dressing ingredients in a screw-topped jar and shake well to combine. Taste and adjust the seasoning if necessary. Pour a little of the dressing over the salad leaves and toss gently. Divide the dressed leaves between four plates and top with the scallops and their corals. Spoon over the remaining dressing; garnish with julienne of lime and serve at once.

Serves 4

## INGREDIENTS

1 round lettuce
2 sticks celery
1 tangerine and 1 grapefruit or 2 ugli fruit
1 small paw paw
2 teaspoons finely sliced Scotch Bonnet pepper
Dressing:
1 teaspoon allspice berries
4 tablespoons sunflower oil
1 tablespoon white wine vinegar
1 tablespoon freshly chopped thyme
1 tablespoon paw paw seeds
salt and freshly ground black pepper

## METHOD

Preparation time: 20 minutes

Remove any damaged, outer leaves from the lettuce and discard them. Wash and dry the remaining leaves and tear the larger ones into bite-sized pieces. Place the lettuce in a large bowl and slice the celery into thin matchsticks and add these to the lettuce.

Peel the ugli fruit using a small, sharp knife and cut in between the membranes to separate the flesh into segments. Add these to the salad bowl. Peel the paw paw and halve it. Scoop out the seeds and reserve 1 tablespoon. Cut the flesh into neat chunks and add it to the salad, together with the sliced Scotch Bonnet pepper. (Scotch Bonnet peppers are very hot Jamaican peppers. Always remove the seeds before using and substitute fresh chillies if they are unavailable.)

Crush the allspice berries in a pestle and mortar and place them in a screw-topped jar with the other dressing ingredients. Shake well to combine and taste and adjust the seasoning if necessary. Pour the dressing over the salad, toss gently and serve at once.

NOTE:
Ugli fruit is a Jamaican citrus fruit which is a cross between a Seville orange, a tangerine and a grapefruit. 1 tangerine and 1 grapefruit can be substituted.

Serves 4

# ROJAK (MALAYSIAN SALAD)

## INGREDIENTS

½ small pineapple
½ small cucumber
1 unripe mango
85 g (3 oz/½ cup) canned water
   chestnuts
1 small guava
55 g (2 oz/½ cup) beansprouts
115 g (4 oz/½ cup) yellow-skinned
   beancurd
vegetable oil for deep-frying
1 tablespoon toasted sesame seeds to
   garnish
(see p.61 for sauce ingredients)

METHOD                                    Preparation time: 30 minutes

For the sauce, soak the tamarind in 150 ml (¼ pint/⅔ cup) boiling water, breaking up the pulp with a spoon and stirring well. Strain, pressing the pulp against the sieve to extract as much flavour as possible. Discard the dry pulp and reserve the liquid for the sauce.

Place the shrimp paste in a small pan and dry-fry it for 1 minute until it is fragrant. Add the crushed chillies and fry for a further minute. Dry-fry the peanuts in a large frying pan (skillet), stirring constantly, until they are golden (about 2 minutes). Tip them into a food processor and dry-fry the sesame seeds for 2 minutes. Add these to the food processor along with the shrimp paste and chilli mixture.

Process the ingredients until finely ground. Add the tamarind liquid and the remaining sauce ingredients and process again for 1 minute. Transfer the sauce to a pan and cook, stirring occasionally, for 3 minutes. Set it aside to cool.

Peel the pineapple, remove the core and cut it into neat chunks. Halve the cucumber lengthways and slice it into diagonal pieces. Peel the mango and cut the flesh into chunks. Halve the water chestnuts lengthways to produce thin discs. Peel the guava, cut away the seeds and dice the flesh.

Blanch the beansprouts for a few seconds in boiling water. Drain and refresh them. Slice the beancurd into small cubes. Deep-fry it in hot oil for about 30 seconds until it is crisp and golden. Drain it on paper towels.

Arrange all the prepared ingredients in separate groups on a large platter, spoon some of the sauce into the centre of the dish and sprinkle with the toasted sesame seeds. Serve the salad, passing the remaining sauce separately.

Serves 8

*Sauce:*
*30 g (1 oz) fresh tamarind*
*1 tablespoon dry shrimp paste*
*1 tablespoon crushed dried chillies*
*115 g (4 oz) raw unsalted peanuts*
*25g (1 oz) sesame seeds*
*juice of 1 lime*
*1½ teaspoons caster (superfine)*
*  sugar*
*1 tablespoon black prawn paste*
*1 tablespoon sweet black sauce*
*pinch of salt*

*To produce the authentic flavour of this salad several specialist ingredients are required. These can be obtained from a good Oriental supermarket. This salad can be served as a starter before an Asian meal.*

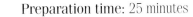

## INGREDIENTS

*450 g (1 lb) cleaned fresh squid*
*salt and freshly ground black pepper*
*2 tablespoons groundnut oil*
*275 g (10 oz) Chinese cabbage*
*small handful of coriander (cilantro)*
*  leaves*
*1 ripe mango*
*1 green pepper (capsicum)*
*Dressing:*
*6 tablespoons groundnut oil*
*2 tablespoons lemon juice*
*2 tablespoons finely chopped shallot*
*4 teaspoons Thai fish sauce*
*2 tablespoons freshly chopped*
*  coriander (cilantro)*
*1 tablespoon freshly chopped mint*
*2 teaspoons finely chopped red chilli*
*pinch of sugar*

## METHOD

**Preparation time:** 25 minutes

Wash and dry the squid, slice it into rings and season lightly with salt and pepper. Heat the oil in a wok and stir-fry the squid rings until they have turned white and are just cooked (about 5 minutes). Remove them from the wok with a slotted spoon and drain them on paper towels.

Peel the mango and cut the flesh away from the stone. Dice the flesh neatly. Cut the pepper (capsicum) in half, remove the core and slice the flesh into diamonds. Place the ingredients for the dressing in a small bowl and whisk together until thoroughly combined. Taste and adjust the seasoning if necessary. Wash and dry the Chinese cabbage and break the leaves into bite-sized pieces. Place them in a large bowl with the coriander (cilantro) leaves.

Pour a little of the dressing over the salad leaves, toss well to combine and line a shallow bowl with the dressed leaves. Place the squid, diced mango and green pepper in a bowl and pour over the remaining dressing. Toss to combine and spoon the squid mixture on to the salad leaves. Serve at once.

Serves 4

# CREOLE SALAD

## INGREDIENTS

225 g (8 oz) basmati rice
1 aubergine (eggplant), about 275 g
  (10 oz)
1 tablespoon olive oil
115 g (4 oz) cherry tomatoes
1 orange pepper (capsicum)
1 small onion
200 g (7 oz) can sweetcorn
Dressing:
4 tablespoons olive oil
2 tablespoons white wine vinegar
3 tablespoons freshly chopped thyme
2 teaspoons paprika
1 clove garlic, crushed
sea salt and freshly ground black
  pepper

## METHOD

Preparation time: 20 minutes

Wash the rice and cook it in boiling salted water until it is tender (about 10–12 minutes). Drain and refresh. Cut the aubergine (eggplant) lengthways into thick slices and brush both sides with olive oil. Cook the slices under a hot grill (broiler) for 6 minutes on each side until crisp and golden. Leave to cool; then cut them into large dice.

Halve the cherry tomatoes. Halve the pepper (capsicum), remove the core and seeds and dice the flesh. Peel the onion and slice it thinly. Drain the sweetcorn. Place the rice and all the prepared vegetables in a large bowl.

Place the dressing ingredients in a screw-topped jar and shake well. Pour the dressing over the ingredients in the bowl and toss to combine. Taste and adjust the seasoning if necessary and, if time, cover and refrigerate for 1 hour before serving to allow the flavours to develop.

Serves 6

# GADOH GADOH (INDONESIAN SALAD)

## INGREDIENTS

*55 g (2 oz/½ cup) yellow-skinned*
*  bean curd*
*30 g (1 oz) raw prawn crackers*
*oil for deep-frying*
*55 g (2 oz/½ cup) beansprouts*
*225 g (8 oz/2 cups) potato, peeled*
*  and diced*
*55 g (2 oz/½ cup) Asian long beans*
*  or French (green) beans*
*55 g (2 oz/½ cup) white cabbage*
*¼ cucumber*
*115 g (4 oz/1 cup) iceberg lettuce*
*2 hard-boiled eggs, peeled*
*(see p.65 for sauce ingredients)*

METHOD                                          Preparation time: 30 minutes

Place the first six sauce ingredients in a food processor and blend to a smooth paste. Heat the oil in a saucepan and fry the paste until it is fragrant (about 3 minutes). Crush the peanuts in the food processor and add them to the pan along with the remaining sauce ingredients. Cook for 4–5 minutes, stirring occasionally. Taste and adjust the seasoning if necessary and allow to cool.

Slice the beancurd into thin strips. Deep-fry it in hot oil for 30 seconds until crisp and golden. Remove it with a slotted spoon and drain on paper towels. Deep-fry the prawn crackers in the hot oil for a few seconds until they turn white and puff up. Remove them with a slotted spoon and drain on paper towels.

Blanch the beansprouts for a few seconds in boiling water. Drain and refresh them in cold water. Cook the potato in boiling water until it is tender (about 5 minutes). Drain and refresh it. Cut the beans into 2.5 cm (1 in) pieces and blanch them in boiling, salted water. Drain and refresh them.

Shred the cabbage finely and blanch it for a few seconds. Drain and refresh it. Cut the cucumber into thin slices and, stacking several slices on top of each other, cut across the slices to produce thin 'green tipped' strips.

To serve, shred the lettuce finely and place it in a shallow serving dish. Toss together the beancurd, beansprouts, potato, beans, cabbage and cucumber in a bowl, and spoon this mixture over the lettuce.

Spoon over the peanut sauce, garnish with quartered hard-boiled eggs and slices of chilli and scatter the prawn crackers on top and around the edges of the bowl. Serve immediately.

**Serves 6**

*Peanut Sauce:*
*2.5 cm (1 in) piece galangal, peeled*
  *and chopped*
*1 small stalk lemon grass, finely*
  *chopped*
*1 small red chilli, seeded and chopped*
*1 clove garlic, crushed*
*2 shallots, peeled and chopped*
*2 teaspoons dry shrimp paste*
*2 tablespoons vegetable oil*
*115 g (4 oz/1 cup) salted peanuts*
*1 tablespoon caster (superfine) sugar*
*1 tablespoon lime juice*
*150 ml (¼ pint) coconut milk*

*Galangal looks similar to root ginger but the skin is whitish and thinner, tinged with pink. If fresh galangal is unavailable, use the powder version substituting a teaspoon of powder for the fresh galangal.*

# ACAR (MALAYSIAN MIXED VEGETABLE SALAD)

## INGREDIENTS

*4 small carrots*
*1 cucumber*
*1 small cauliflower*
*115 g (4 oz) French (green) beans*
*225 g (8 oz) white cabbage*
*2 large red chillies*
*2 large green chillies*
*10 small shallots*
*300 ml (½ pint/¼ cup) cider vinegar*
*30–55 g (1–2 oz) caster (superfine)*
  *sugar*
*3 tablespoons sunflower oil*
*4 cloves garlic, crushed*
*1 tablespoon chilli powder*
*1 tablespoon turmeric*
*½–1 teaspoon salt*
*175 g (6 oz/1¼ cups) salted peanuts*
*85 g (3 oz/¾ cup) toasted sesame*
  *seeds*

## METHOD

**Preparation time:** 25 minutes

Peel the carrots and cut them into thin 5 cm (2 in) sticks. Cut the cucumber lengthways into quarters, cut away the seeds and slice the flesh into thin 5 cm (2 in) sticks. Divide the cauliflower into florets. Top and tail the beans and halve them. Shred the cabbage finely. Cut the chillies lengthways into quarters and remove the seeds. Peel the shallots and leave them whole.

Place the vinegar and 300 ml (½ pint/1¼ cups of water in a saucepan and bring to the boil. Blanch the different vegetables in separate batches, cooking each batch for 1-2 minutes, depending on the type of vegetable. Remove each batch with a slotted spoon and place them in a large mixing bowl. Stir in the sugar and set aside.

Heat the oil in a small pan and fry the garlic until it is golden. Mix the chilli powder and turmeric with 2 tablespoons of water to make a paste and add to the garlic. Cook slowly for about 5 minutes, stirring constantly to prevent the mixture from burning. Stir in the salt and set it aside to cool. Crush the peanuts coarsely and add to the vegetables with the cooled chilli mixture and sesame seeds. Mix well and refrigerate overnight before serving.

Serves 6–8

## INGREDIENTS

*225 g (8 oz) broccoli*
*225 g (8 oz) courgettes (zucchini)*
*55 g (2 oz/½ cup) raw cashew nuts*
*1 tablespoon sunflower oil*
*¼ teaspoon chilli powder*
*a little sea salt*
*2 tablespoons coconut chips*
*Curry Mayonnaise:*
*55 g (2 oz/½ cup) mayonnaise*
*1 tablespoon plain yoghurt*
*1 tablespoon mango chutney*
*2 teaspoons hot curry paste*

## METHOD

Preparation time: 20 minutes

Divide the broccoli into small florets and cook them in a pan of boiling, salted water for 3 minutes. Drain and refresh them in cold water. Cut the courgettes (zucchini) into 5 cm (2") sticks and cook them in a pan of boiling, salted water for 1–2 minutes. Drain, refresh and set aside.

Heat the oil in a frying pan (skillet) and stir-fry the cashew nuts for 1–2 minutes until golden. Remove them with a slotted spoon, drain on paper towels, then tip them into a bowl and sprinkle over the chilli powder and sea salt. Toss well to combine. Dry-fry the coconut chips for 30 seconds until pale golden. Transfer them to a bowl and leave to cool.

Place the mayonnaise ingredients in a small bowl and mix well to combine. Place the broccoli, courgettes and half the cashew nuts in a serving bowl, pour over the mayonnaise and toss gently. Scatter over the remaining nuts and the toasted coconut and serve immediately.

Serves 4

# THAI BEEF SALAD

## INGREDIENTS

*450 g (1 lb) fillet of beef*
*115 g (4 oz) baby spinach leaves*
*8 radishes, sliced thinly*
*4 spring onions (scallions)*
*½ cucumber*
*3 tablespoons rice vinegar*
*4 teaspoons soy sauce*
*5 tablespoons sunflower oil*
*pinch of sugar*
*Marinade:*
*2 teaspoons chilli bean sauce*
*2 tablespoons Thai fish sauce*
*juice of 2 limes*
*2.5 cm (1 in) piece fresh ginger root,*
*  peeled and finely chopped*
*4 cloves garlic, crushed*

## METHOD

**Preparation time:** 30 minutes

Place the marinade ingredients in a small bowl and whisk to combine thoroughly. Wipe the beef and cut it into 1.25 cm (½ in) slices. Lay the slices of beef in a shallow glass dish, pour over the marinade, cover and refrigerate for at least 2 hours.

Crush the garlic and place it in a small bowl. Add the remaining dressing ingredients and mix well to combine. Taste and adjust the seasoning if necessary. Cover the dressing and refrigerate it until it is required.

Wash the spinach leaves and dry them in a salad spinner. Break off any large stalks and place the spinach in a mixing bowl. Wash the radishes and slice them thinly, and add them to the spinach. Remove the green parts of the spring onions (scallions) and slice the white parts diagonally. Peel the cucumber and dice it. Add these to the bowl and set aside.

To make garnish tassels, trim away most of the green part of the spring onions and discard. With a small pair of scissors, make small cuts from one end of each spring onion, about halfway along the length. When they are all cut into fine strips, place them in a bowl of ice cold water and refrigerate to allow the ends to curl.

Place the rice vinegar, soy sauce, 4 tablespoons of the sunflower oil and sugar in a small bowl. Whisk thoroughly to combine and set aside. Remove the beef from the marinade and heat the remaining sunflower oil in a large pan. Cook the meat in two batches, for 1–2 minutes on each side.

Allow the beef to rest and then cut it into thin strips. Toss the beef strips in the beef dressing. Add the rice vinegar dressing to the spinach leaves and toss lightly. Line a shallow serving bowl with the dressed spinach. Spoon the beef mixture into the centre, garnish with the spring onion tassels and serve immediately.

Serves 4-6

*Beef Dressing:*
*2 cloves garlic*
*juice 2 limes*
*2 tablespoons chilli sauce*
*2 teaspoons chopped ginger root*
*2 teaspoons chopped green chilli*
*4 teaspoons freshly chopped*
  *coriander (cilantro)*

CUCUMBER FANS (shown opposite)
Halve a cucumber lengthways. Place it cut side down on a board and make several fine diagonal cuts in the cucumber, cutting almost to the end of each slice. Bend alternate slices inwards to create loops.

VAN DYKE RADISHES
(shown opposite)
Using a small, sharp knife make a series of deep zig-zag incisions around the upper edge of each radish. When you have cut all the way round, gently pull apart the two pieces. The tops can also be used for garnishing.

# JAPANESE SALAD

### INGREDIENTS

*30 g (1 oz/½ cup) arame seaweed*
*1 teaspoon sesame oil*
*½ cucumber*
*a little salt*
*55 g (2 oz/½ cup) mooli (white radish)*
*2 large carrots*
*few slices of Japanese pickled ginger to garnish*
*Dressing:*
*2 tablespoons rice vinegar*
*2 tablespoons sesame oil*
*3 teaspoons shoyu (Japanese soy sauce)*
*1 tablespoon sake*

## METHOD

**Preparation time:** 25 minutes

Rinse the seaweed and soak it in a bowl of water for 5 minutes. Remove, reserving the water, and sauté the seaweed for 1–2 minutes in the sesame oil. Pour the water into a saucepan, add the seaweed and simmer, covered, for 35 minutes until it is tender. Drain and set it aside.

Use a canelle knife to make ridged patterns in the cucumber skin, then slice it very thinly, sprinkle with a little salt and place it in a colander to remove the moisture. Set aside for 30 minutes. Peel the mooli and slice it thinly diagonally. Rinse the cucumber and pat it dry on paper towels.

Peel the carrots and use the canelle knife to make five ridges along the length of each carrot. Slice the carrots thinly to produce 'flowers'. Mix the dressing ingredients together until thoroughly combined. To serve, arrange decorative circles of seaweed, carrot, cucumber and mooli on individual plates. Spoon a little dressing over each plate and garnish each portion with a few slivers of pickled ginger. Serve immediately.

**Serves 4–6**

# CRISPY DUCK AND MANGO SALAD

## INGREDIENTS

*2 large Barbary duck breasts, about
350 g (12 oz) each*
*1 tablespoon olive oil*
*1 medium mango, peeled and cubed*
*85 g (3 oz/³⁄₄ cup) Macadamia nuts*
*225 g (8 oz ) baby spinach leaves,
washed and dried*
*Curried Mayonnaise:*
*175 ml (6 fl oz/³⁄₄ cup) mayonnaise*
*2 teaspoons mild curry paste*
*1 teaspoon lemon juice*
*2 tablespoons milk*
*1 teaspoon mango chutney*
*salt and freshly ground black pepper*

## METHOD

**Preparation time:** 20 minutes

Cut each duck breast in half
lengthways and cut each half into thin
slices. Heat the oil in a heavy-based
frying pan (skillet) and cook the duck
strips in two batches, cooking each
batch until crisp and golden (about 10
minutes). Remove with a slotted
spoon and drain on paper towels.
Allow to cool slightly.

Place all the mayonnaise ingredients
together in a bowl and mix well.
Season to taste. Just before serving,
add the duck strips, mango and
Macadamia nuts to the mayonnaise.
Toss to combine.

Divide the spinach leaves between
four large plates and place a quarter
of the duck mixture in the centre of
each plate. Serve immediately.

Serves 4

## INGREDIENTS

450 g (1 lb) skinned, boned chicken breast
1 cos (romaine) lettuce
1 cucumber, peeled
*Tikka Marinade:*
1 small onion and 1 clove garlic, chopped
1 tablespoon chopped ginger root
1 teaspoon each of ground coriander,
  ground cumin and garam masala
½ teaspoon salt, turmeric and chilli
  powder
3 tablespoons plain yoghurt
2 tablespoons lemon juice
2 tablespoons chopped coriander (cilantro)
*Dressing:*
4 tablespoons plain yoghurt
2 tablespoons freshly chopped mint
1 tablespoon white wine vinegar
½ teaspoon sugar

## METHOD

Preparation time: 25 minutes

Cut the chicken into 2.5 cm (1 in) cubes and place in a bowl. Place the marinade ingredients in a food processor and blend to a smooth paste. Toss the chicken cubes in the paste until they are well coated. Cover and refrigerate, preferably overnight, or for several hours before cooking.

Place the dressing ingredients in a small bowl and mix well to combine. Taste and adjust the seasoning if necessary and refrigerate until needed. Thread the chicken on to 8 skewers and cook under a preheated grill (broiler), turning once, until the chicken is cooked (about 12–15 minutes). Set aside.

Discard any damaged, outer leaves from the lettuce and wash and dry the remaining leaves. Cut the cucumber in half and use a swivel peeler to produce 'ribbons' of cucumber, discarding the central 'core' of seeds. Arrange the lettuce leaves and cucumber ribbons on four plates, place two chicken skewers on each plate and drizzle a little dressing over each portion. Garnish with mint sprigs and serve immediately, passing the extra dressing separately.

Serves 4

# AVOCADO SALAD WITH MARINATED PEPPERS

### INGREDIENTS

*450 g (1 lb) asparagus*
*1 small red batavia lettuce or similar*
*55 g (2 oz) marinated peppers*
   *(capsicums) in brine*
*4 tablespoons walnut pieces*
*2 large avocados*
*2 teaspoons lemon juice*
*focaccia or olive bread to serve*
*Dressing:*
*4 tablespoons walnut oil*
*1 tablespoon red wine vinegar*
*1 teaspoon French mustard*
*sea salt and freshly ground black*
   *pepper*
*pinch of sugar*

METHOD                                Preparation time: 30 minutes

Trim the woody ends from the asparagus stalks and use a vegetable peeler to peel the outer layer of the stalks up to the tips. Cut the asparagus into 5 cm (2 in) pieces and blanch them in a pan of boiling, salted water for 2 minutes. Drain and refresh in cold water.

Separate the lettuce into leaves and break it into bite-sized pieces. Wash the salad and dry it in a salad spinner or between clean tea towels (dish cloths). Drain the peppers (capsicums) and cut them into long thin strips.

Toast the walnuts lightly by dry-frying them in a small pan over a medium heat, stirring constantly to prevent them from burning. When they look deep brown (after about 2–3 minutes), transfer them to a plate and leave to cool.

Peel the avocados with a small sharp knife. Halve them and remove the stones (pits). Cut the flesh into thin slices and place them on a large plate. Sprinkle over the lemon juice to prevent discoloration.

Place all the dressing ingredients in a small bowl and whisk together until thoroughly combined. Taste and adjust the seasoning if necessary and set aside until required.

To serve, divide the lettuce between four plates. Arrange the avocado and asparagus on top of the lettuce and add some pepper strips to the centre of each plate. Scatter over the walnuts, spoon some dressing over each salad and serve immediately with warm bread.

Serves 4

*Focaccia is olive oil flat bread from Genoa in Italy. It is delicious served with salads, soups or just eaten on its own. The picture on the right shows plain focaccia, along with two of the flavoured versions: onion and garlic and herb.*

# LOBSTER SALAD

## INGREDIENTS

*2 large freshly cooked lobsters*
*1 pink grapefruit*
*½ ripe peach*
*55 g (2 oz/½ cup) seedless red*
*  grapes*
*85 g (3 oz) frisée lettuce*
*Dressing:*
*1 shallot, finely chopped*
*1 clove garlic, crushed*
*2 teaspoons freshly chopped chervil*
*2 teaspoons freshly chopped tarragon*
*6 tablespoons light olive oil*
*2 tablespoons champagne vinegar*
*sea salt and freshly ground black*
*  pepper*

METHOD

Preparation time: 30 minutes

Remove the lobster heads and break off the large claws. Lay the lobster tail on its back and use scissors or a sharp knife to cut down on either side of the shell. Remove the tail flesh and slice it into thick discs. Crack the claws with a mallet and remove the flesh. Cut it into bite-sized pieces.

Place all the ingredients for the dressing in a small bowl and whisk to combine. Taste and adjust the seasoning if necessary. Peel the grapefruit with a small sharp knife and divide it into segments, cutting in between the membranes. Slice the peach and halve any large grapes. Wash and dry the frisée lettuce.

Divide the frisée between two dinner plates. Arrange the lobster and prepared fruit on the beds of lettuce. Spoon the dressing over each salad and serve at once.

NOTE:
Frozen cooked lobster tails can be bought from speciality shops and are more economical than cooked fresh lobster but are not, of course, as flavoursome.

Serves 2

# SMOKED TROUT AND BEETROOT SALAD

## INGREDIENTS

*350 g (12 oz) mixed salad leaves*
  *such as lollo rosso, frilice, chervil*
  *and oak leaf lettuce*
*6 smoked trout fillets*
*350 g (12 oz) cooked beetroot*
*shiso or mustard and cress to garnish*
*Dressing:*
*8 tablespoons soured cream*
*4 teaspoons horseradish sauce*
*4 tablespoons virgin olive oil*
*sea salt and freshly ground black*
  *pepper*

## METHOD

**Preparation time:** 20 minutes

Place all the dressing ingredients in a small bowl and mix well to combine. Season to taste and refrigerate to allow the flavours to develop. Wash and dry the lettuce leaves and tear any large ones into quarters.

Lay the trout fillets on a board and divide each fillet in half lengthways using a sharp knife. Slice the beetroot into neat circles.

To serve, divide the salad leaves between four plates. Arrange three halves of trout fillet on each plate and divide the beetroot between the plates. Spoon over the creamy dressing and garnish with shiso or mustard and cress. Serve immediately.

NOTE:
Shiso looks similar to mustard and cress except that the leaves are purple and more pointed. It has a mild 'aniseed' flavour.

Serves 4

# *Tofu, Egg and Mushroom Salad*

### INGREDIENTS

*2 eggs*
*2 teaspoons vegetable oil*
*225 g (8 oz/1 cup) smoked tofu bean*
  *curd*
*145 g (5 oz) oyster mushrooms*
*1 orange pepper (capsicum)*
*175 g (6 oz/1½ cups) sprouted*
  *lentils*
*8 baby sweetcorn*
*1 small lollo rosso lettuce*
*Dressing:*
*3 tablespoons groundnut oil*
*1 tablespoon sherry vinegar*
*1 tablespoon light soy sauce*
*1 tablespoon freshly chopped ginger*
  *root*
*1 spring onion (scallion), thinly sliced*
*1 teaspoon clear honey*
*salt and freshly ground black pepper*

METHOD

Preparation time: 30 minutes

Beat the eggs with salt and pepper until well combined. Heat 1 teaspoon of the oil in a frying pan (skillet) and pour in the egg mixture. Cook until it is golden on the underside and cooked in the centre. Transfer the omelette to a plate and allow it to cool.

Brush the tofu all over with the remaining teaspoon of oil. Place it under a moderately hot grill (broiler) and cook it, turning once, until it is golden (about 10 minutes). Leave to cool, then slice it into 12 pieces.

Wipe the mushrooms to clean them and slice any that are large. Place them in a large bowl. Halve the pepper (capsicum) and remove the core. Cut the flesh into diamond shapes and add these to the mushrooms.

Roll up the omelette and slice it thinly into long strips. Add these to the bowl along with the sprouted lentils and baby sweet corn that have been halved lengthways.

Wash and dry the lettuce leaves and tear them into bite-sized pieces. Place all the dressing ingredients in a screw-topped jar and shake well to combine. Taste and adjust the seasoning if necessary.

To serve, divide the salad leaves between four plates. Pour three-quarters of the dressing over the prepared ingredients in the large bowl and toss lightly to combine. Spoon this mixture over the lettuce, lay three slices of tofu over each portion, and spoon over the remaining dressing.

Serves 4

VARIATION:

Try varying the flavour of this salad by using the alternative ingredients listed below for the dressing.

*3 tablespoons sesame oil*
*1 tablespoon sherry vinegar*
*1 tablespoon light soya sauce*
*1 clove garlic, peeled and finely*
*  chopped*
*1 tablespoon freshly chopped*
*  ginger*
*1 small green chilli, de-seeded*
*  and finely chopped*
*1 teaspoon clear honey*
*salt and ground black pepper*

# GRILLED LETTUCE SALAD

## INGREDIENTS

300 g (11 oz) mild French goat's
  cheese
4 teaspoons freshly chopped thyme
sea salt and freshly ground black
  pepper
4 Little Gem lettuces
1 tablespoon olive oil
225 g (8 oz) mixed red and yellow
  cherry tomatoes
Dressing:
4 tablespoons olive oil
4 teaspoons white wine vinegar
4 teaspoons Italian black olive paste
salt and freshly ground black pepper

## METHOD

**Preparation time:** 30 minutes

Combine all the dressing ingredients
in a small bowl and whisk to combine
thoroughly. Season to taste and set
aside. Place the goat's cheese and
thyme in a small bowl, season with
salt and pepper and mix well to
combine. Taste and adjust the
seasoning if necessary.

Discard any damaged outer leaves
from the lettuces and halve each
lettuce lengthways. Use a small sharp
knife to hollow out the heart of each
lettuce half. Brush each half with
olive oil and spoon the cheese and
thyme mixture into the hollows. Cook
under a hot grill (broiler) until the
cheese begins to brown (about 8–10
minutes), then set them aside to cool.

Wash, dry and halve the tomatoes.
Divide them between four serving
plates. Add two Little Gem halves to
each plate and drizzle over a little of
the dressing. Spoon the remaining
dressing generously over the cherry
tomatoes and serve immediately.

**Serves 4**

# PORK, PRUNE AND PISTACHIO SALAD

## INGREDIENTS

*115 g (4 oz) lollo blando lettuce*
*1 punnet shiso*
*350 g (12 oz) pork fillet*
*sea salt and freshly ground black*
  *pepper*
*1 tablespoon sunflower oil*
*115 g (4 oz) slim courgettes*
  *(zucchini), halved lengthways*
*1 tablespoon pistachio nuts*
*6 ready-to-eat dried prunes,*
  *quartered*
*4 dried apricots, cut into slivers*
*Dressing:*
*½ teaspoon saffron threads*
*3 tablespoons set plain yoghurt*
*2 tablespoons sunflower oil*
*2 teaspoons cider vinegar*
*sea salt and freshly ground black*
  *pepper*

## METHOD

Preparation time: 25 minutes

Soak the saffron threads in 2 teaspoons of boiling water and leave to infuse for 5 minutes. Separate the lettuce into leaves and wash and dry them. Cut the stems of the shiso away from the roots. Wash and dry the stems and discard the roots. Place the dressing ingredients in a bowl and stir in the saffron strands and water. Whisk well to produce a smooth dressing. Taste and adjust the seasoning if necessary.

Slice the pork into 2.5 cm (1 in) pieces and season it well. Heat the oil and fry the pork in two batches until it is cooked through and golden (about 5 minutes). Transfer to a bowl and leave to cool.

Slice the courgette (zucchini) halves thickly and blanch them in boiling, salted water for 1 minute. Drain and refresh them and add them to the pork along with the pistachios, prunes and apricots. Pour over the dressing and toss well to combine. Line a shallow serving bowl with the lettuce and shiso and spoon the pork mixture into the centre. Serve at once.

Serves 4

## INGREDIENTS

*20 large raw king prawns (shrimp) in
  the shell*
*30 g (1 oz/2 tablespoons) butter*
*225 g (8 oz) mixed salad leaves*
*1 tablespoon sesame seeds*
*175 g (6 oz) baby sweetcorn*
*1 tablespoon sesame oil*
*4 bananas*
*4 tablespoons fresh lime juice*
*Seasoning:*
*½ teaspoon salt*
*2 tablespoons paprika*
*2 teaspoons cayenne pepper*
*2 tablespoons dried fines herbes*
*2 teaspoons garlic granules*
*2 teaspoons dried onion granules*
*Dressing:*
*4 tablespoons sesame oil*
*2 tablespoons fresh lime juice*
*½ teaspoon sugar*

## METHOD

**Preparation time:** 30 minutes

Remove the heads and shells from the prawns (shrimp). Using a pair of scissors, cut each prawn almost in half down to the tail, making sure that it still holds together in one piece. Place the seasoning ingredients in a bowl and mix well to combine.

Melt the butter in a small pan and using a pastry brush 'paint' each prawn with butter and then dip it in the seasoning mixture to coat well.

Heat a large cast-iron frying pan (skillet) until it is smoking. Sprinkle a few drops of water on to the surface: if they 'dance', it is hot enough to start cooking. Cook the prawns in three batches, cooking them for 1½–2 minutes on each side until they are 'blackened'. Set them aside to cool.

Wash and dry the salad leaves and herbs. Tear them into bite-sized pieces and place them in a large bowl. Dry-fry the sesame seeds in a small pan for 2 minutes, stirring constantly until they are toasted. Transfer them to a bowl to cool.

Blanch the corn in boiling, salted water for 1 minute. Drain them and then brush them with the sesame oil and sprinkle with sea salt. Cook them under a hot grill (broiler) for 5 minutes on each side until lightly charred. Slice the bananas and toss them in the lime juice. Grill them for 3 minutes on each side until lightly charred.

Add the dressing ingredients to the sesame seeds and whisk to combine. Pour the dressing over the salad leaves and toss well. Divide the dressed leaves between four plates. Add five prawns to each plate along with a quarter of the char-grilled corn and banana. Serve immediately.

**Serves 4**

VARIATION:

'Blackening', the method used to cook the prawns, is a very popular style of cooking in the American South. Vary this recipe with 'blackened' chicken, using 4 skinless, boneless chicken breasts. Place one chicken breast at a time between sheets of cling film and beat with a rolling pin until the flesh is about 5 mm (¼ in) thick. Paint the chicken breasts with melted butter and dip in the spice mixture as described in the recipe above. Cook the chicken breasts in the same way as the prawns, but increase the cooking time to four minutes per side.

## INGREDIENTS

*350 g (12 oz) fresh white crabmeat*
*2 large oranges*
*12 sprigs chervil*
*2 bunches watercress*
*20 medium chicory (endive) leaves*
*Dressing:*
*3 tablespoons crème fraîche*
*1 tablespoon champagne vinegar*
*1 tablespoon reserved grated orange*
*   zest*
*3 tablespoons grapeseed oil*
*sea salt and freshly ground black*
*   pepper*

## METHOD

Preparation time: 20 minutes

Flake the crabmeat and place it in a bowl. Using a zester, remove 1 tablespoon of zest from one of the oranges and set it aside for the dressing, then peel both oranges with a small, sharp knife and divide them into segments, cutting in between the membranes. Add the segments to the crabmeat with the chervil sprigs.

Remove any tough stalks from the watercress and break it into bite-sized pieces. Wash and dry the watercress and chicory (endive) leaves and set them aside.

Place the dressing ingredients in a screw-topped jar and shake well to combine. Taste and adjust the seasoning if necessary. Line a shallow salad bowl with the watercress and chicory. Pile the crabmeat and orange mixture into the centre, spoon over the dressing and serve immediately.

Serves 4

84

# MONKFISH AND FENNEL SALAD

## INGREDIENTS

800 g (1 lb 11 oz) monkfish
  (goosefish)
salt and freshly ground black pepper
2 tablespoons olive oil
2 small red peppers (capsicums)
8 cloves garlic, unpeeled
450 g (1 lb) fennel
1 tablespoon lemon juice
175 g (6 oz) escarole lettuce
Dressing:
6 tablespoons olive oil
3 tablespoons balsamic vinegar
2 tablespoons finely chopped fennel
  fronds
sea salt and freshly ground black
  pepper

## METHOD

Preparation time: 25 minutes

Remove all the membrane from the monkfish (goosefish) and cut the flesh away from the central bone. Wash and dry the pieces of fish, season them with salt and pepper and place them in a small roasting tin with the olive oil. Halve the peppers and remove the cores. Place the peppers (capsicums) and the cloves of garlic on a baking sheet. Pre-heat the oven to 200°C (400°F/gas 6). Bake the fish for about 20 minutes and the peppers and garlic for about 25 minutes. Remove and set aside to cool.

Remove the fronds from the fennel and reserve for the dressing. Slice the fennel thinly and blanch it for 2–3 minutes in a pan of water to which the lemon juice has been added. Drain and refresh it in cold water. Place the dressing ingredients in a screw-topped jar and shake well to combine. Season to taste. Wash and dry the lettuce leaves and tear them into bite-sized pieces.

Slice the cooled monkfish into bite-sized pieces and place them in a bowl. Cut the peppers into thick strips, removing skins if desired, and add these to the bowl with the fennel. Peel the baked garlic and cut each clove into quarters. Add them to the bowl. Pour over the dressing and toss well to combine. Arrange the lettuce leaves on four serving plates. Divide the fish mixture between the four plates and serve at once.

Serves 4

# WARM SEAFOOD SALAD

## INGREDIENTS

*1 litre (1³/₄ pints/4¹/₄ cups) fish stock*
*2 large sprigs fresh tarragon*
*225 g (8 oz) cleaned squid*
*16 raw prawns (shrimp) in the shell*
*450 g (1 lb) mussels, scrubbed*
*175 g (6 oz) frisée lettuce*
*175 g (6 oz) escarole lettuce*
*Dressing:*
*4 tablespoons virgin olive oil*
*1 tablespoon tarragon vinegar*
*1 tablespoon freshly chopped*
 *tarragon*
*1 teaspoon freshly chopped chives*
*2 teaspoons coarse-grain mustard*
*salt and freshly ground black pepper*
*pinch of sugar*

## METHOD

Preparation time: 25 minutes

Place the fish stock and tarragon in a large pan and bring it to a simmer. Slice the squid into rings and poach it in the stock for 2 minutes. Remove with a slotted spoon and set aside. Repeat the process with, first, the prawns (shrimp), until the shells turn pink (about 2 minutes) and then the mussels, until their shells open (also about 2 minutes).

Reserve 8 mussels in their shells. Peel the prawns and remove the remaining mussels from their shells. Add them to the squid rings. Wash and dry the lettuce and tear it into bite-sized pieces.

Divide the lettuce leaves between four plates. Add a quarter of the mixed seafood to each plate. Place the dressing ingredients in a small saucepan and warm through gently. Spoon the warm dressing over the seafood, garnish each plate with 2 mussels in their shells and serve at once.

Serves 4

# – 7 –
# ON THE SIDE

# BEETROOT AND ORANGE SALAD

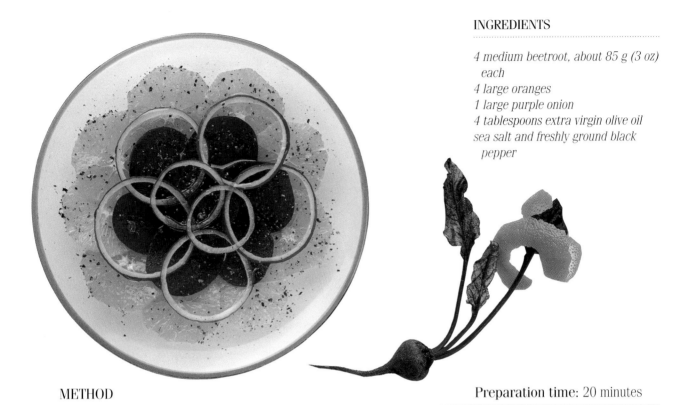

### INGREDIENTS

*4 medium beetroot, about 85 g (3 oz)
  each*
*4 large oranges*
*1 large purple onion*
*4 tablespoons extra virgin olive oil*
*sea salt and freshly ground black
  pepper*

METHOD

Preparation time: 20 minutes

Remove any leaf stalks from the beetroot but do not trim off the tapering roots. Wash them carefully, taking care to keep the skins intact so they do not 'bleed' while cooking. Cook in salted water until they are tender (about 1-1½ hours). When the beetroot are cool, peel off their skins.

Using a small sharp knife remove the skin and pith from the oranges, then slice each orange thinly into rings. Peel the onion and slice it thinly. Separate the slices into rings.

To serve, slice each beetroot and arrange on a plate with one of the sliced oranges. Scatter some onion rings over each portion and drizzle over 1 tablespoon of olive oil. Season generously with salt and pepper and serve at once.

NOTE:
To save time, the beetroot can be bought ready-cooked and peeled from most large supermarkets. Allow about 85 g (3 oz) beetroot per person.

**Serves 4**

# AVOCADO AND WATERCRESS SALAD

## INGREDIENTS

2 bunches watercress
2 avocados
1 tablespoon lemon juice
Dressing:
1 lemon
6 tablespoons grapeseed oil
1 teaspoon Dijon mustard
½ teaspoon clear honey

## METHOD

Preparation time: 15 minutes

Using a zester, pare 1 teaspoon of lemon zest from the lemon and reserve it. Squeeze the juice and place all the dressing ingredients in a screw-topped jar. Shake well to combine. Taste and adjust the seasoning, adding more honey if necessary then set aside.

Remove any thick stalks and the roots from the watercress. Break the leaves and young stalks into small bite-sized pieces and wash and dry them. Peel the avocados, halve them and remove the stones (pits). Then slice them thickly and place in a small bowl with the lemon juice to prevent discoloration.

To serve, place the avocado and the watercress in a salad bowl, pour over the dressing and toss gently to combine. Scatter over the reserved lemon zest and serve the salad immediately.

Serves 4

# BEAN AND PEA SALAD

## INGREDIENTS

*175 g (6 oz) thin French (green)*
  *beans*
*410 g (14 oz) can petits pois*
*3 spring onions (scallions)*
*Garlic Mayonnaise:*
*125 ml (4 fl oz/½ cup) mayonnaise*
*1 clove garlic, crushed*
*2 tablespoons freshly chopped*
  *parsley*
*2 tablespoons milk*
*½ teaspoon sea salt*
*½ teaspoon caster (superfine) sugar*
*freshly ground black pepper*

## METHOD

**Preparation time: 25 minutes**

Top and tail the beans and cut them into 2.5 cm (1 in) pieces. Cook them in a pan of boiling, salted water until they are cooked but still crisp (about 5 minutes). Drain and refresh them in cold water and place them in a large bowl.

Drain the petits pois and add them to the beans. Wash and trim the spring onions (scallions) and slice them thinly on the diagonal. Add these to the bowl.

Place all the ingredients for the garlic mayonnaise in a small bowl and mix well to combine. Taste and adjust the seasoning if necessary. Add the mayonnaise to the peas and beans and toss until all the vegetables are well coated. Transfer to a serving bowl and if time permits, leave to stand for 30 minutes to allow the flavours to develop.

**Serves 4**

# CARROT AND MOOLI SALAD

## INGREDIENTS

350 g (12 oz) carrots
350 g (12 oz) mooli (white radish)
4 tablespoons raisins
*Vinaigrette:*
1 tablespoon cumin seeds
4 tablespoons sunflower oil
4 teaspoons rice wine vinegar
½ teaspoon chilli powder
sea salt and freshly ground black
  pepper

## METHOD

Preparation time: 25 minutes

Trim the ends from the carrots and mooli and peel them. Using a swivel vegetable peeler shave long 'ribbons' from the carrots and mooli and place them in a bowl. Stir in the raisins and set aside.

Dry-fry the cumin seeds in a small pan for 1–2 minutes until they begin to 'pop', then transfer them to a small bowl and add the remaining vinaigrette ingredients.

Whisk together until thoroughly combined. Taste and adjust the seasoning if necessary and pour over the carrot and mooli. Toss well to combine and if time permits, leave to stand for 30 minutes to allow the flavours to develop.

NOTE:
Try adding 2 tablespoons of pistachio nuts to this salad for an interesting variation.

Serves 6

## INGREDIENTS

*175 g (6 oz) mixed green salad
  leaves such as cos, frisée and oak
  leaf lettuces*
*55 g (2 oz) mangetout (snow peas)*
*½ large green pepper (capsicum)*
*2 sticks celery*
*basil sprigs to garnish*
*Fresh Herb Dressing:*
*4 tablespoons olive oil*
*4 teaspoons champagne vinegar*
*1 tablespoon freshly chopped parsley*
*1 tablespoon freshly chopped basil*
*1 tablespoon freshly chopped chervil*
*sea salt and freshly ground black
  pepper*
*pinch of sugar*

## METHOD

**Preparation time:** 20 minutes

Wash and dry the salad leaves and tear them into bite-sized pieces. Place them in a large bowl. Top and tail, and halve the mangetout (snow peas). Blanch them in boiling, salted water for 30 seconds, drain and refresh them under cold water and add them to the lettuce leaves.

Remove the core from the pepper (capsicum) and slice it into long thin strips. Slice the celery on the diagonal and add both of these to the bowl of salad leaves.

Place the dressing ingredients in a screw-topped jar and shake well to combine. Toss the dressing through the salad and serve immediately in individual bowls, garnished with a sprig of basil.

Serves 4

# SALAD LEAVES WITH ROASTED PEPPER DRESSING

## INGREDIENTS

*20 medium chicory (endive) leaves*
*12 medium radicchio leaves*
*3 hard-boiled eggs, peeled and sliced*
*12 black olives*
*Pepper Dressing:*
*1 medium red pepper (capsicum),*
*    quartered*
*1 large red chilli*
*1 tablespoon olive oil*
*1 small shallot, chopped*
*1 clove garlic, chopped*
*2 tomatoes, skinned, seeded and*
*    chopped*
*2 tablespoons mayonnaise*
*sea salt and freshly ground black*
*    pepper*

## METHOD

Preparation time: 30 minutes

Place the pepper (capsicum) and chilli under a hot grill (broiler) for 10–15 minutes until charred on all sides. Allow them to cool, then remove the skins and seeds and chop the flesh roughly.

Heat the olive oil in a frying pan (skillet). Add the shallot and garlic and cook for 3–4 minutes, then add the tomatoes and cook for a further 2 minutes until the mixture is soft. Leave to cool and then place in a food processor together with the pepper and chilli and blend to a smooth purée. Add the mayonnaise, salt and pepper and blend again briefly. Taste and adjust the seasoning if necessary.

To serve, wash and dry the salad leaves and divide them between four plates. Spoon over the dressing and top with slices of egg and the olives.

**Serves 4**

## INGREDIENTS

450 g (1 lb) baby new potatoes
225 g (8 oz) brown cap button
   mushrooms
½ cucumber
Mustard Mayonnnaise:
4 tablespoons mayonnaise
4 tablespoons creme fraiche
2 teaspoons coarse-grain mustard
sea salt and freshly ground black
   pepper
pinch of sugar

## METHOD

Preparation time: 20 minutes

Scrub the potatoes and cook them in a pan of boiling, salted water until they are tender (about 12 minutes). Drain and refresh them under cold water and slice each potato in half. Place them in a large bowl. Wipe and trim the mushrooms and halve any that are large. Add them to the potatoes.

Peel the cucumber and halve it lengthways. Using a teaspoon scoop out the seeds and slice the flesh into half-moon shapes. Add to the potatoes and mushrooms. Place the ingredients for the mayonnaise in a bowl and mix well to combine.

Add the mayonnaise to the potatoes, mushrooms and cucumber and toss well to ensure that everything is well coated. Taste and adjust the seasoning if necessary, then leave to stand for 1 hour before serving to allow the flavours to develop.

Serves 6

# 'GREEN GODDESS' SALAD

## INGREDIENTS

*225 g (8 oz) mixed salad leaves such
    as lollo rosso, frilice and rougette
    lettuce*
*Dressing:*
*2 anchovy fillets, finely chopped*
*2 tablespoons freshly chopped
    tarragon*
*1 tablespoon freshly snipped chives*
*1 tablespoon freshly chopped parsley*
*150 ml (¼ pint/⅔ cup) mayonnaise*
*1 tablespoon tarragon vinegar*
*1 tablespoon water*
*sea salt and freshly ground black
    pepper*

## METHOD

Preparation time: 15 minutes

Place the chopped anchovy fillets in a bowl with the herbs, mayonnaise, vinegar and water and mix well to combine. Season lightly with salt (as the anchovies are salty) and black pepper.

Wash the salad leaves and dry them in a salad spinner. Tear the larger leaves into bite-sized pieces.

Toss together the salad leaves and dressing in a large bowl and serve immediately on individual plates.

Serves 4